How to De-Junk Your Life

Written by Dawn Dwyer
Edited by National Press Publications

NATIONAL PRESS PUBLICATIONS

A Division of Rockhurst College Continuing Education Center, Inc.
6901 West 63rd Street • P.O. Box 2949 • Shawnee Mission, Kansas 66201-1349
1-800-258-7248 • 1-913-432-7755

National Press Publications endorses nonsexist language. In an effort to make this handbook clear, consistent and easy to read, we have used "he" throughout the odd-numbered chapters, and "she" throughout the even-numbered chapters. The copy is not intended to be sexist.

How to De-Junk Your Life

Published by National Press Publications, Inc.
Copyright 1998 National Press Publications, Inc.
A Division of Rockhurst College Continuing Education Center, Inc.

Printed in the United States of America

12 13 14 15 16

ISBN 1-55852-222-0

Table of Contents

INTRODUCTION

"De-junking my life? Do I have to throw away all my treasures?"

"If I could find it, you could have it!"

"I know I need to get control of my desk!"

"My home's a mess, and I can't find anything in a hurry."

"I can find it eventually — it just takes time to locate what I need."

"I think I'm pretty organized, but I'm sure I could do better."

If you've ever made at least one of these statements, then this book is for you. And if you're like most people, you feel like you need to get organized. Don't panic! De-junking your life is possible. I know it's possible because I've had success in de-junking my life.

I'm not by nature one of those neat, orderly, well-organized people. In fact, when I first started helping organizations and people de-junk their lives, I had a family member who nearly fell off her chair laughing. "You?! Helping people de-junk their lives?!" She reacted this way because I'd always been the one in our family who kept everything. I hung on to teaching materials, books, half-finished art projects, pictures, mementos from trips, treasures the kids brought home from school — you name it and I had it somewhere!

At work I had stacks of files and piles of paper on my desk. I was afraid to put them away because I thought I'd forget about the work that I had to finish. My middle desk drawer was always empty during the day so I could just sweep things off my desk into that drawer each night. That way I'd know where everything was the next morning. Then it would take me 10 to 15 minutes every morning just to get everything out of the drawer so I could start working.

One day I realized I spent more time getting ready to work than it actually took to complete a task. I had to spend so much time finding things because I was disorganized and had too much junk in my life. So I declared war on junk. As I got my professional life under control, it was such a great feeling that I started de-junking my personal life. Even though I've been working on this for several years, I'm still not finished. However, I'm more successful and have less stress and more balance in my life since I started my war on junk.

JAKE will help

How have I managed to wage the war? I have a helper, JAKE, which stands for Junk Always Kills Effectiveness. JAKE's a happy warrior because he loves helping people get rid of junk. He goes to war wearing his combat helmet in order to survive throwing things away. He has night-vision goggles so he can see junk in the darkest corners of desk drawers, behind file cabinets and in storage areas. He also finds junk in the attic, basement, closets and other dark areas at home. His combat boots are for kicking junk loose, no matter how long it's been there. He's armed with wastebaskets, trash bags and recycle bins, which makes it easier to haul the junk away.

JAKE's a great junk warrior who will be with you all through this book. Each time you meet JAKE, remember to watch for the junk that interferes with your success. JAKE will also give his Top Ten at the end of each chapter. These lists are great tools to jump-start your war on junk!

What JAKE won't give you are checklists of things to have in each room or specific tools to use. The reason JAKE doesn't do that is because only you know exactly how you work, how you live and what you need to be successful.

In fact, let's start the war by defining junk. In this book, junk means anything that clutters up your life and interferes with your success, productivity and effectiveness. It might be furniture you don't need or use any longer. It might be too many commitments junking up your time. It might be papers that are out of date or priorities that are out of balance. Anything that interferes with your success is junk.

Organize for success

De-junking isn't the same for every person. One person's organization may be another person's chaos. Some people like a very structured lifestyle, with every detail written down so they have a sense of control over each day. Others are more comfortable in a less structured environment. So there's not one best way to get organized to de-junk your life.

You need to decide what degree of organization is necessary for you to be successful. I don't define success by how much money you earn, how neat your home is or how high up the corporate ladder you climb. I believe true success is feeling positive about yourself and being productive both professionally and personally.

Benefits from the war

As you begin to de-junk your life, get organized and focus on the things that are truly important to you, you'll see at least five benefits:

- You'll have a sense of control over your life.

- You'll find it easier to get things done.

- You'll have less stress in your life.

- You'll have time for the things you want to do.

- You'll be more productive.

Now good luck in winning your war on junk!

1 LET'S GET STARTED!

How do you start your war on junk? You'll need a battle plan to get moving in the right direction. As you begin your war, remember this isn't something you'll have to do only once. It's a process that gets easier as you become more experienced with de-junking. It's also a process that lasts a lifetime because it's so easy to continue adding junk to your life.

Baby steps

De-junking requires baby steps. In the movie *What About Bob?*, Bob was a guy whose life was a mess, but he wanted to straighten it out all at once. His psychiatrist kept telling him to use "baby steps, baby steps." Bob wasn't very successful because he wasn't patient and he didn't take things slowly.

So remember these baby steps when you begin de-junking your life. Select the area you want to de-junk first and use baby steps to get started. Don't try to straighten out everything all at once because it'll be too frustrating and stressful. You may even give up on your war before the first battle's won. Take it one baby step at a time. You didn't junk up your life overnight, and you won't correct the problem overnight. Remember baby steps, baby steps!

You'll need to be aware of your tendency to let junk into your life. In this book, I'll deal with four major areas of life that seem to be problems for most of us.

1. Space

2. Paper and electronic information

3. Time

4. Priorities

Since these cause problems both at work and at home, I'll deal with the professional and then the personal aspects in each area.

Pick one

Don't try to attack everything at once. Pick one area you want to concentrate on and go to that section of the book for immediate help. There you'll find principles, tips, tools and suggestions. Select one and implement it. When you're comfortable with that first change, go back and select another from that same section of the book or another section. Think of this book as a resource to keep at your fingertips. You'll be able to refer to it again and again as you wage your war on junk.

Make an appointment with yourself to start de-junking. Begin by setting aside one hour. At the end of the hour, stop, even if you're not done. You can then realistically look at what you've started and decide if you need to continue today or make another appointment.

Junk collects in four areas: space, paper and other information, time and priorities. Decide which area you want to deal with first. What two things are your greatest concerns in this area? Write them down here.

Area to concentrate on:

1.

2.

Reflections
Reflections

Three important questions

As you consider each kind of junk — whether it's space, information, time or priorities — ask yourself these three questions:

1. Why do I need this in my life?

2. Why do I want this in my life?

3. Why is this essential to my life?

Learn to ask "why" in your war on junk. This forces you to evaluate why you need something or why you need to do something. If you simply ask, "Do I need this?" the answer is almost always "yes!" So use "why" to help you get to the real issue.

Choices and more choices

We live in a world with lots of choices. Although it's wonderful to have choices, they make it too easy to add junk to your life. Think of all the options that you have every day. Even going to the grocery store for bread gives you choices beyond your imagination. You have to choose from among wheat, white, oat nut, rye, sourdough, etc. The list's almost endless.

Also consider your options when buying a car. Now there are auto malls with several dealers in one place. They sell cars in different colors and sizes: compact, mid-size, full-size, sport-utility vehicle, van, mini-van and pick-up truck, to name just a few. You can even add optional equipment to your vehicle. Choices like these are repeated over and over in our lives. Because having so many choices can junk up your life, it's time to think about getting organized.

Left brain/right brain

The way you get organized depends partially on how you process information. People who think in a linear fashion are very organized, methodical and logical. These are usually left-brain people. Right-brain people are generally more creative and haphazard. They use lateral thinking, which consists of unrelated thought patterns. Of course, the environment you're raised in and the environment you work in each day also plays a part. If you're a left-brain person raised in a right-brain environment without a great deal of structure, you won't be as organized as a left-brain person raised in a left-brain environment.

I'm a right-brain person who lives professionally in a left-brain environment. I conduct training events, meet clients, handle multiple projects and constantly live by airline schedules, travel arrangements and time frames my profession imposes on me. I was raised in a left-brain environment. This makes it easier for me to function as a left-brain person professionally. That doesn't mean I arrange my professional life by the same guidelines as a left-brain person who was raised left-brain and lives left-brain. Does that make me right and the other person wrong? Absolutely not!! Remember, we're all unique and different. Take the information in this book, adapt it, modify it and just ignore some of it because it won't work for you. If you're wondering which side of the brain you use most, here's a tool to help you.

How Do You Think?

Do you ...		Do you...
• Try to find new ways to look at things?	3 2 1 4 5 6	• Try to find absolutes when judging issues?
• Avoid looking for "right" or "wrong" answers?	3 2 1 4 5 6	• Seek "yes" or "no" justification?
• Analyze ideas to determine "how"?	3 2 1 4 5 6	• Analyze ideas to determine "why"?
• Become concerned with change and movement	3 2 1 4 5 6	• Become concerned with stability?
• Make illogical jumps from one step to another?	3 2 1 4 5 6	• Make logical jumps from one step to another?
• Welcome intrusions of information	3 2 1 4 5 6	• Selectively choose what to consider?
• Consider what is irrelevant?	3 2 1 4 5 6	• Consider the relevant only?
• Progress by avoiding the obvious?	3 2 1 4 5 6	• Progress by using established patterns?
• Avoid guarantees?	3 2 1 4 5 6	• Guarantee at least minimal standards?

Total the numbers you circled: _____

Scoring and interpretation

This is a fun tool to use because there are no right or wrong answers. You'll notice there are two columns of questions with numbers between them. There's also a line drawn down the middle of the page that divides the numbers. Read both of the questions and decide which one is most like you — the question on the left or the question on the right. Once you've made your choice, score yourself on the question you've selected. If you selected the question on the left, your choices will be 1, 2 or 3. If you selected the question on the right, your choices will be 4, 5 or 6. After you've made your choices and scored each question, add all the numbers together and write the total on the page.

Remember there's no "superior" or "best" way to respond. This is only a tool to help you understand your natural tendencies. The more you understand yourself, the easier it is for you to function effectively and successfully. The higher your score, the more likely you are to use the left side of your brain. Right-brain people generally have lower scores. However, few people function with just one side of their brains. Instead, they use a combination of left- and right-brain skills to process information, but they have a predominant side. Some people have equal access, which means they use both sides of the brain equally. Part of the time they use the linear, left-brain approach, and other times they use the creative, right-brain approach.

If your score is 26 to 38, you probably have equal access in processing information. A score of 9 to 25 indicates a right-brain person, and 39 to 54 indicates a left-brain person. This doesn't have anything to do with your intelligence or whether you are right-handed or left-handed. It only indicates how you process information most of the time.

Left-brain people are usually:

- Positive
- Concrete
- Analytical
- Rational
- Linear
- Active
- Explicit
- Goal-oriented
- Sequential
- Verbal

Right-brain people are generally:

- Intuitive
- Holistic
- Spontaneous
- Playful
- Emotional
- Talkative
- Nonverbal
- Symbolic
- Visual
- Physical
- Artistic

Equal-access people generally have a combination of attributes from both lists and move easily from using one side of the brain to the other.

You can use this information to help you de-junk your life more effectively. As you make changes, make the ones that fit your natural tendencies and build on your strengths. Don't try to use a detailed calendar if you're predominately a right-brain person because this will frustrate you. If you're primarily a left-brain person, you might feel like things are out of control without a detailed calendar.

The left-brain person usually likes neat, tidy, well-organized surroundings. Right-brain people are more likely to be surrounded with chaos — piles, boxes and even bags of information — but they can generally find things in their mess. An equal-access person can easily move between the two categories, so they have more choices in de-junking their lives. This also means it may be harder for them to settle on the things that are really important to them. For instance, an equal-access person might like a very detailed calendar like a left-brain person, but he or she also might arrange a workspace with more flair and change it more often like a right-brain person.

After completing the left-brain/right-brain assessment, evaluate yourself and mark on the line below where you see yourself. Assess how your natural tendencies helped you junk up your life. Consider how you can use your strengths to de-junk your life.

1____2____3____4____5____6____7____8____9____10____

No junk in my life   *Lots of junk in my life*

Which of my tendencies help me junk up my life?

Which of my strengths will help me de-junk my life?

Summary

As you start waging your war on junk, find the degree of organization that's best for you — one size definitely doesn't fit all when it comes to de-junking. You'll need to decide which of the four areas — space, paper and electronic information, time or priorities — you want to deal with first and go to that section of the book. As you use the three questions, take baby steps and work with JAKE, you'll start a life-long process that will help you be more successful and have less stress and more balance in your life. The benefits can be enormous if you're willing to declare war on junk. Here's JAKE's Top Ten to help you get started NOW!

JAKE's Top Ten

1. Be yourself — don't try to be someone else.

2. Determine which area you want to tackle first:

   - Space (See Chapters 2 and 3.)

   - Paper and other types of information (Turn to Chapters 4 and 5.)

   - Time (Check out Chapters 6 and 7.)

   - Priorities (Go to Chapter 8.)

3. Answer the "three" questions to help you de-junk your life.

4. Take baby steps.

5. Be aware of your left-brain/right-brain tendencies.

6. Use your strengths to be effective.

7. Work with JAKE.

8. Don't change everything at once.

9. Realize this is a lifelong process.

10. Get started now.

Read the appropriate chapter for your first area of concern. Then make an appointment to start the de-junking process. Mark this appointment on your calendar. (If you don't have a calendar, write the appointment down somewhere so you don't forget it.) In the space below, write down what things you'll de-junk first. Remember to take baby steps!

Reflections

2 JAKE AT WORK

A client came to me for help with his office space. He had a small office with two file cabinets, a desk with a left-hand extension, some bookshelves and two chairs, one on each side of the desk. He didn't like walking around the left-hand extension every time he wanted to leave the office or get something from his files. He didn't have any windows, and the only door was located in one corner of his office. I suggested he turn the desk around so the extension wouldn't be in his way when he left the room.

It was an "aha" experience for him. "You're right," he said. "All I have to do is turn my desk around and that solves the problem. Why didn't I see that?" Since he used another office to meet with clients, he got rid of one of the chairs. Remember JAKE suggests simplifying and eliminating anything without a purpose.

You've all had experiences like this man. Someone else can come into your situation and immediately see what needs to be done. This happens because you adapt to your circumstances, which can be both positive and negative. Adaptability is a wonderful trait, however, it can lead you to accept less-than-ideal settings or circumstances. This is why it's often easier for outsiders to see things that need to be changed. Their minds aren't cluttered with "how it's always been."

Is it permanent?

One common problem with workspace is that it seems so permanent. Your motto may be "I've always done it that way!" or "It's always been that way!" Maybe you inherited your workspace from someone else and you haven't made any changes.

At least once a year, ask yourself these questions about your workspace:

1. Have your job responsibilities changed in the last year?

2. Do you have items in your workspace you don't use?

3. What items do you need to do your job more effectively?

4. Is your workspace arranged for maximum performance?

5. Has the traffic flow changed in the last 12 months?

6. Do you have enough storage space (or any storage space)?

7. Where is the equipment you use located? Do you have enough space for the equipment you use constantly or consistently?

8. Do you meet with others during the course of your workday — clients, suppliers, co-workers, etc.? Does your workspace allow you to work effectively with other people?

As you answer these questions, you may discover you need to de-junk your workspace. Some of you may work in manufacturing areas, cubicles or shared workspaces. Regardless of your type of workspace, you need to assess how effective it is for you.

Don't be concerned about how someone else has her workspace arranged, unless you think the arrangement would help you be more effective. Peter Drucker, author of several management books, says it's more important to be effective than to be efficient. This is particularly true in terms of workspace. Look for the arrangement that will help you be most effective, the one that's best suited to your work style. Always evaluate your workspace by asking, "Is there a better way for me to arrange this?"

Arranging your workspace

There are several ways you can arrange your workspace. One way is the traditional L-shape.

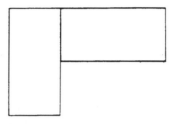

In this arrangement, the desk usually has an extension (either right- or left-hand) that forms a right angle and creates an L shape. If arranged correctly, this gives you two work areas. Instead of using a desk extension, you could get the same effect using a desk with a table. The desk is usually the prime working space, and the extension or table is secondary.

You might use the extension for your computer equipment and its drawers for your computer supplies. If you make a lot of phone calls, it also might be used as a telephone center. Set it up so you have easy access to your call sheets, customer or client files, pens or pencils, notepad and any other items you need for making calls. The extension is also a good place for doing research.

Another arrangement is the U-shape, where the desk serves as the focal point for the work area and it has two extensions.

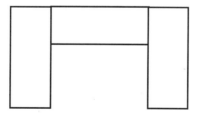

With this arrangement, the desk usually has an extension on one side and a table or computer workspace on the other side. Or, there might be file cabinets instead of computer workspace.

A parallel arrangement could also work for you and the space you have.

In this arrangement, your two major work surfaces are parallel to each other. If you need a large workspace, you might try two tables instead of a desk and table. Just remember to examine your work habits and work style and then arrange your office to complement your natural tendencies.

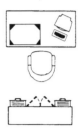

Two offices

Another possibility is to have two separate work areas if space and your budget allow. If you deal with the public, you might want an office that's professional looking and easy for conversation. In your separate work area, you can keep your computer equipment, research projects, reference materials and the tools you need for your job at your fingertips. With this arrangement, there's no need to worry about your office being "too cluttered" to meet with clients.

Cubicles

For those of you who work in cubicles, you usually can't arrange the workspace to fit your individual work personality. That means the "neatnik" will have the same workspace arrangement as the "chaos champ." However, the neatnik often searches for tools to help organize her space, while the chaos champ usually gets along with what's already there.

Try these organizational tools to help you de-junk your workspace. For example, there are shelves that hang from the top of the cubicle wall, velcro picture frames and modular furniture pieces that maximize space. Don't overdo the gadgets, but check out what's available by periodically taking a stroll through an office supply store. Even if you have to purchase these yourself, they'll be worth it if you improve your effectiveness.

Make a list of absolutely everything you need to do your job. Then look around your workspace and throw everything else away.

If there's something on the list you need and don't have, make plans now to get it. Write your plan below.

Reflections
Reflections

Furniture

First, look for ways to maximize the space you have, whether it's a large corner office or a small cubicle. Each piece of furniture should have a purpose beyond just looking good.

If you have a credenza, use it for storage. Store current projects in folders on top of the credenza. Use vertical file holders to keep files upright rather than horizontal. They'll look more professional, be easier to find and make good use of the space. Use the inside of the credenza to store materials you refer to frequently or other items best left hidden away, such as computer disks and supplies. Store supplies in clear containers so it's easy to see when you need to reorder.

File cabinets

File cabinets shouldn't be kept in your workspace unless you need to refer to them on a regular basis. Otherwise, store your file cabinets somewhere else and keep your workspace for day-to-day or ongoing work. File cabinets can become collectors for things you don't really need or use. Clean them out periodically or even eliminate them, if possible. Whenever possible, store documents on computer disk instead.

Your desk

Since a desk is necessary in most work areas, look for one with lots of drawer space. I like a desk that has a large drawer on one side for a tickler file, which I consider vital in most work situations. The tickler file is a place to put anything that has a date or deadline so you won't miss it. (I'll explain more about a tickler file in Chapter 4.) Also be cautious about desk accessories. They may add things to your desk that you don't need or use and actually interfere with your effectiveness.

The wastebasket

You absolutely must have a wastebasket. It may seem funny to even mention it, but this is one of the very best tools you have for de-junking your life. Recycling bins should also be within easy access. And if you have a large workspace, you might need two wastebaskets and recycling bins.

Separate work areas

If you have a large office, you may want separate work areas for various tasks. For example:

- It may be better to have a specific area for all of your computer equipment, supplies and software. It could be easily accessible from your desk by simply swinging your chair around.

- You may need another area for telephoning if you have regular contact with clients, customers or suppliers. You could keep all your customer files, order information and telephone supplies in this area.

- If you do lots of research, a large table may be a necessary addition to your office. This would allow you to spread out all of your materials.

- If you frequently meet with people in your office, set up a small round table and chairs in a corner away from your desk.

Evaluate your workload and work assignments and let them determine the type of furniture you need in your office. Don't copy what someone else has in her work area. Find what works for you and eliminate the rest. This is your workspace, so make sure it fits your work needs and your personality, even if you have the same job as the person next door.

Your computer

A separate table is a good idea for your computer equipment. If you're right-handed, place your computer equipment to the left of your desk. If you're left-handed, place it on the right. This makes it easier for you to reach things on your desk when you're using your computer. Here are some other tips:

- Use a copy stand to hold the material you're working on.

- Try a mouse platform that fits on the arm of your chair and gives relief to your wrist.

- Use an anti-glare screen to reduce eyestrain and glare.

- Change your keyboard if you're not comfortable with the touch or sound of its keys. Keyboards aren't expensive, so purchasing a new one may be well worth it for the added comfort.

Remember, when you're comfortable with your working conditions, it lowers your stress level, raises your productivity and de-junks your life.

Space-savers

If you have a small workspace, consider the following:

- Vertical wall-storage units for your paper files. They give you easy access to information and keep it organized and looking professional.

- A wall telephone. This saves desk space and still provides easy access.

- A headset to free your hands while you're on the telephone. This saves your neck and shoulders from wear and tear. It also allows you to do two things at once.

- Hot pockets or hot files. These attach to the wall and hold folders, papers and other projects so they're off your desk, eliminating clutter.

- Hanging picture frames. These also reduce desk clutter.

- Bulletin boards. These are great for displaying charts, memos, news clips and other temporary items.

Space-wasters

I can't give you a list of what you need in your workspace because everyone's work style and type of work is different. However, here's a list of things you don't need because they tend to junk up your workspace. Just remember to follow this rule: If you don't use it, dump it.

1. Obsolete equipment. Times change, needs change, equipment changes — so get rid of that wonderful old adding machine your great-grandfather was the last one to use.

2. Desk accessories you don't use. They look great, but if they add to the clutter and you don't use them, get them off your desk.

3. Anything that's broken. Some items to watch for include calculators, staples, chairs, file cabinets, clocks, answering machines, computers, monitors and printers. Although this isn't a complete list, it alerts you to the items that are most likely to break down.

4. Excess office furniture. Some offices seem to collect extras: chairs, tables, typing stands, magazine racks, shelves never used or even installed. These things may be good, but they should be dumped if they're not being used. If you occasionally need an extra chair, consider a folding chair kept out of sight. By doing this, it makes it harder for people to drop by your office, then sit and visit.

5. Souvenirs. If you have too many, toss them. Instead, showcase something that expresses who you are. Don't collect things that are hard to dust or display. If possible, put them in a case so they don't appear old, dirty and junky.

6. Computer clutter. This includes computer diskettes, CD-roms, software, manuals, cords, printers, paper in different types and sizes, etc. Get rid of disks with outdated programs or those you can't access because of hardware or software changes. The list goes on and on.

7. Homey touches. It's possible to have too many pictures and other personal items. Your workspace isn't a recreation area or a family room. It needs to reflect a professional image, with just a few personal touches to let your clients, co-workers and others know you have a life outside your work.

8. Old sticky notes. I have nothing against sticky notes. However, some workspaces look like sticky note factories because they're everywhere. Keep them to a minimum and throw them away when you're finished with them.

9. Anything obsolete, unusable, unnecessary or that slows down your ability to function effectively. Weed it out of your workspace. Be ruthless and dump it!

If it's too hard for you to eliminate some of these treasures, get a "clutter buddy" to help you. Since it's always easier to throw away someone else's junk, your best ally may be a clutter buddy who can be ruthless about your stuff. Of course, it would probably be easier for you to throw away that person's junk too. Try forming an anti-clutter team and help everyone de-junk his or her work areas.

Look at what's left in your workplace and decide the best way to arrange it to fit your needs. Carefully evaluate where to place your furniture. Make sure the arrangement fits your work assignment and your work style.

In the space below, draw a diagram of an arrangement that would suit your specific needs.

Reflections
Reflections

Summary

It's important to arrange your workspace for maximum effectiveness. At least once a year evaluate your work responsibilities and your workspace. Be willing to rearrange your furniture or eliminate some of it. If you work in a small area, look for space savers to help you be more effective. Remember, if you don't use it, dump it! A great ally in your war on junk may be a clutter buddy who will help you clean up your work space. Remember to let JAKE help you with your war on work-related junk. Here's his Top Ten just for you.

JAKE's Top Ten

1. Ask someone else to evaluate your workspace.

2. Check the message your workspace sends.

3. Display professional awards, certificates, etc. in your workspace.

4. Rearrange your workspace so you're more productive.

5. Decide what you need to eliminate so you have less stress at work.

6. Ask the eight questions about your workspace at least once a year.

7. Enlist a clutter buddy to help you de-junk.

8. Conquer computer clutter by periodically cleaning out this area.

9. Have one or more wastebaskets and recycling bins.

10. If you don't use it, dump it!

3 JAKE AT HOME

Ever have one of those mornings when you overslept, didn't know what you were going to wear, and once you grabbed something out of the closet you couldn't find the brown belt to go with those tan slacks? Then, after your shower, you stumbled over two pairs of shoes trying to get to your blow dryer, which was in the back of a cabinet with its cord tangled up with a toothpaste tube, razor, and some cotton swabs. Sound familiar? Some of you may have mornings like this because you haven't de-junked your home space. If that's the case, it's time to call in JAKE!

De-junking your personal space can have the same benefits as de-junking your professional space. When you eliminate things you don't need, don't use or that have worn out or don't work, life becomes simpler, with less stress and more balance. You're able to focus on other things. Regardless of how small or large your home may be, you can de-junk it. You can get more enjoyment out of your personal space as a result of getting rid of things.

It's not easy

I believe this is one of the hardest areas of your life to de-junk. In going through your home, you're looking at tangibles — things you can handle, look at and in some cases, even hear and smell. You may have a squeaky old rocker that belonged to your great-grandmother, and you're not about to get rid of it. Or you may have some Depression glass that your family has used all your life. You're going to keep it because you can't imagine not having it around. If it means something to you, then it's important.

The trick is discovering what's really important to you. It's easy for some people to get caught up in collecting "stuff" just for the sake of collecting. They collect things that will probably never appreciate in value and that have no personal meaning to them. They just like to collect "stuff."

Collectibles or clutter?

If you're going to collect something, decide what you'll collect, why you're collecting it and how you'll display it. When you're standing at the edge of the Grand Canyon that souvenir salt and pepper shaker set may seem like the perfect collectible. Then you think, "I could collect a set of salt and pepper shakers to remember each place I visit." Great idea, but where will you keep these wonderful sets if you live in a small, one-bedroom apartment? Someone who has an extra bedroom could have shelves built just to display all the salt and pepper shakers. Instead, you might say, "I'll collect one set every three years." Then you can control the number of collectible items and enjoy deciding which ones you really want.

A caution about collectibles

Be careful about what you collect. You might create a monster you can't control. I know a woman who, as a teenager, started collecting anything with pigs on it because she thought it was unique and cute. Fifteen years later, she's drowning in pigs. Whenever people think of her they say, "Karla loves pigs, so let's get her something with pigs on it."

Even with collectibles you really enjoy, you need to remember JAKE. Make sure you have a good reason for your collection. If you aren't careful, collectibles become just another way of adding junk and clutter to your life.

Take some time now to list any collections you have. Are you ready to let go of any of them? If not, why?

Make sure you have a proper place to display or store your collectibles. If you don't have a specific place, write down a plan to establish one.

Reflections

Where to start?

If you try to de-junk your whole house all at once, it'll be too overwhelming. You may quit without finishing the job. Tackle just one room at a time, starting with the area that's most frustrating to you. Get that under control and then move on to another problem area.

Begin with the bathroom

The bathroom is a good place to start because it's usually one of the smallest rooms in the house and it's easier to de-junk than a larger room. Also you use this area soon after getting out of bed. I know some of you run to the kitchen for a cup of coffee or breakfast before you start getting ready for the day, but sooner or later you end up in the bathroom.

Walk into your bathroom and take a good look around. You should see things that are pleasing to you: colors, shapes and accessories. Remember only the people who use the bathroom have to be pleased with its overall appearance. I have a friend who's a great Raiders football fan, and his bathroom is done completely in silver and black with the Raiders' emblem on the wastebasket and a framed Raiders' poster on the wall. Even though I'm a Raiders fan too, this isn't my idea of the perfect thing to see first thing each morning. But that's okay because it's not my bathroom.

After seeing how pleasing your bathroom is, ask yourself, "How functional is it?" Here are some questions to help you evaluate your bathroom.

1. What are the items you use most?

2. Where are they stored?

3. How easy are they to find each morning?

4. Are they within reach? Keep the items you use most often in top drawers or on shelves that are between eye level and waist level.

5. Why do I even have this item? Is it necessary?

6. Is the clock easy to see? Having a clock lowers your stress level because you can quickly check the time and stay on schedule.

You don't always have a choice about the storage space in your bathroom, however, look for ways to maximize the space you have. In some situations space organizers can be very helpful. Don't overdo them though because they can lead you to store things you don't use or need. Ask yourself, "Is this item really necessary?" Don't ever ask, "Do I want this item?" Instead ask, "Why do I want this item? Will I really use it?" Don't forget JAKE if you're thinking about adding something else to your bathroom.

Arrange your medicine chest with the most often-used items on the bottom shelf or where they're most conveniently stored. A contact wearer told me she always leaves her contact solutions, storage case and other items on the counter beside her bathroom sink. "If I didn't do that I would never be able to find them in the morning because I can't see a thing without my contacts." Of course, homes with young children need to keep safety issues in mind when deciding where to store certain items.

Some things in the bathroom lead a double life. I have a relative who insists the lid to the hair spray can is really a drinking cup. Another person I know has a toothbrush holder with a cup in the middle, and he keeps his toothpaste in that cup.

A basket under the sink may hold cleaning supplies, clean rags and paper towels. That way everything for cleaning the bathroom and for cleaning up spills is handy and easy to reach. Under the sink is not prime storage space because you have to lean over to get to it. However, if that's your only storage space, then organize it with the items you use most in front and others in the back.

Bedroom

Next let's tackle the bedroom, another place people tend to collect stuff they never use. First think about your morning routine during the week.

1. What do you use consistently?

2. What do you stumble over, walk around or have to move when you're getting ready for the day?

3. Do you have too much furniture in the bedroom?

4. Do you have the right furniture in your bedroom?

5. Do you need more storage space?

6. Is there enough light in the bedroom?

First look at the tops of dressers or other storage areas in the bedroom. Are things stacked and piled there? This is something that's a constant problem for me. It's so easy to drop books and other items I'm using for various activities on the dresser. Soon the stacks start to grow.

Instead, it's better to have a place to put things and then be consistent about putting them there. My wise grandmother used to say, "A place for everything and everything in its place," and she was right. Having a place for everything will help de-junk and balance your life. Although it takes discipline to follow through and put things away, you'll never build that discipline if you don't designate somewhere to put them in the first place.

Carefully examine other pieces of furniture in the bedroom. Are there too many knick-knacks sitting around? These slow your ability to clean quickly and efficiently. Could some be mounted on the wall, placed in shadow boxes or glassed in to keep out the dust and cobwebs? Consider hanging pictures on the wall rather than setting them on a dresser. While I certainly don't think you should eliminate all the personal touches in your home, try not to over-do it.

One thing that may end up in the bedroom is exercise equipment. Just remember that exercise bicycle is not a clothes rack. Yes, I do have one in my bedroom. My husband keeps saying he's going to ride the bicycle, so we keep it where it'll be handy to use. I should mention the bicycle has been handy for several years now and is rarely ridden. If you don't regularly use the equipment, move it somewhere else where it's out of the way.

Check the closet

What's in your closet? Take a realistic look. Are there clothes you haven't worn in the last two years? If so, take them to a consignment shop or give them to a charity. Some items in your closet may be too small or too large. You keep thinking they'll eventually fit you. Typically they never do. I know how it is because I've done the same thing. It's time to bring out JAKE's night-vision goggles to find those unworn things that have been lurking in your closet for several seasons.

How is your closet arranged? It should be organized in the way that makes the most sense to you. I have all my pants in one area, tops in the next, followed by skirts, jackets, suits and then dresses. I don't wear dresses as often as the other items so they're in the back of the closet. In my case, how I use an item determines where I store it.

Another option for organizing a closet may be to arrange items by color. That way it's easy to find things that go together. You also could arrange your closet by seasons. Since I live in Southern California where we don't really have seasons, that's not very practical for me. However, when I lived in Northern California, I arranged my clothes by season and by type. Although that arrangement worked for me then, it wouldn't work now. Remember, you need to be willing to change your method of organization when it no longer works or makes sense to you.

Kitchen

Since junk seems to gravitate toward the kitchen, JAKE should take a good, hard look here. Start by thinking about your morning routine. What do you need at your fingertips to help your mornings go smoothly? If you need a caffeine fix first thing in the morning, fill your coffeepot and set the timer before you go to bed. Then your coffee's ready when you get up. If you don't have a coffeepot with a timer, you might want to invest in one. Only you can decide if it's important enough to add a programmable coffeepot to your kitchen. Or, is it just one more item to junk up your space?

Since I'm not a coffee drinker, this wouldn't be important for me. However, I like to eat breakfast, so having those items within easy reach is important. My cereals (hot and cold) are all on shelves I can reach without bending over. Again usage determines storage.

Arrange your kitchen keeping usage in mind — especially what works best for you. Since I'm tall, I put my most commonly used food items on upper shelves. If you're short, you'd probably want to put them on the lower shelves. Always arrange your living space according to your needs — not the way someone else would do it.

Food also can be arranged by how it's used — all the food for main dishes in one area, the dessert items together, snacks in another place and sandwich items close to where sandwiches will be made. Find the arrangement that works best for you and then stick with it. When everything is together, food preparation won't take as much time. And you'll feel less stress because you're not running around the kitchen to get what you need.

How about your counter tops? What's sitting out? Is it something you use frequently or is it just for looks? Anything you use frequently that's not sitting out should be easily retrieved. Some of you like to put everything away: toaster, can opener, coffeepot, food processor and other items. If you like frequently used items out of sight, put them in the front part of your cabinet shelves so you don't have to move other items to get to them. This cuts down on food preparation time.

Where are your utensils? Your pots and pans? Your mixing bowls? Your spices and flavorings? When you're cooking, do you walk from one side of your kitchen to the other just to get everything together? The more you can store items together for a task, the more efficient you'll be. Cups, plates and silverware need to be close to the dishwasher for ease in putting them away. Keep glasses near the sink and/or refrigerator so they're easy to grab when someone needs a drink.

If the kitchen is where you keep your keys, have a key holder right by the outside door. Use a vertical or magnetic file holder for sorting the mail. Give each family member a separate slot so whoever's sorting mail can quickly and easily drop items in each person's slot. These tips get things off the kitchen counter so they don't interfere with food preparation and clean up.

Use a two-tiered space caddy to double the space on a cabinet shelf. It works like a lazy Susan so it's easy to reach the items you've stored. Little baskets can keep things in drawers organized. There are all kinds of wonderful organizers for most problem items so decide what you need and then buy them. Garage sales can be a great place to find these organizers, and the price is usually right! Just think, you might be able to organize your junk drawer without spending a fortune.

Think about your daily routine. What are the stressful times in your day? Record these for five or six days.

Evaluate these stressful times. What can you eliminate or reorganize in your home so you'll have less stress?

Family room

This is the room that usually collects sports equipment, hobby items, magazines, puzzles, books and videos — all those things you use for fun and recreation. Which means JAKE needs to use all his de-junking weapons here, sometimes on a regular basis. Since family rooms usually don't have enough storage space to keep all those items readily available, look for storage cabinets with moveable shelves. This gives you versatility because the shelves can be changed to fit your needs. Also consider investing in a magazine rack with several dividers and special storage racks for videos, CDs and audiocassette tapes. These are available at most discount and office-supply stores.

Many family rooms are used for displaying awards, trophies and special family pictures. Take time to arrange these items in display cases, shadow boxes or on shelves so others can enjoy them. When you receive new items, remove the older ones. By keeping your displays up-to-date and current, it helps de-junk your room. After all, how interesting is it to look at trophies that are five or six years old? Either get rid of the old things or store them out of sight.

Living room

You may keep your living room less cluttered than the rest of the house, but it probably can still be de-junked. Again watch out for displayed items that are old and out of date. Walk into the room and pretend you're seeing it for the first time. What type of message does this room send about you? Is it the message you want to send?

Ask yourself what should be eliminated so the room will be more comfortable and inviting. This doesn't always mean getting rid of old furniture. It may mean rearranging what you have into a cozier setting. For instance, do you have areas that invite conversation? Are the chairs arranged so it's easy for people to see each other? What's the focal point of the room?

If you're having a hard time "seeing" your living room, ask a friend you trust to give you some feedback and suggestions. Another set of eyes often uncovers things you have become so accustomed to that you really don't notice them anymore.

Children's rooms

If you have children, you already know these rooms can accumulate odds and ends very quickly. When a baby is born, everyone brings or sends gifts: stuffed animals, the start of a doll or sports collection, books, tapes, even a tape recorder to a child who isn't a month old. Look carefully at the items you already have in the baby's room or the ones you're thinking about putting there. Since it's hard to de-junk this room once the item gets in, be sure you want it in the first place. If you're thinking of a gift for a baby's room, check with the parents before you assume they'd just love that little treasure you want to add to the nursery.

Periodically go through your children's toys and clothes to get rid of things they no longer use. Don't give your child a new toy without eliminating an older toy first. Let your child choose a charity or another child to receive the used toy. This helps children develop a habit of helping others. It also builds de-junking skills at an early age.

The same thing is true for clothes. Get rid of items that are too small, torn, in need of repair, worn out or just no longer needed. You might have family or friends with whom you can share these clothes. In our extended family, we trade clothes back and forth because the kids are about the same age. It's great to see a special dress or shirt you gave a cousin come back for your own child to wear. These items can also be given to a charity or taken to a consignment shop for resale. You might even make some money!

Keep children's accessories in small containers so they're easy to find. It's better to fill several little boxes or baskets with socks, underwear, belts and other small items and keep them in their drawers than to have all these things dumped in them. You can find these small boxes or baskets in the plastic wares section of many stores.

It's also helpful to arrange your child's closet with matching items together. This makes it easy for younger children to select their own clothes and still look good. It also helps children build self-confidence as they successfully take responsibility for their appearance. Children's closets also can be arranged with pants in one area, shirts in the next and so on.

Children should have a specific place to put away toys and other things. It's difficult to develop a habit of putting things away when there isn't a specific place for them. (Actually, this is true no matter what age you are.) This is why storage crates, bins and clear plastic containers are great for kids rooms.

As a child grows, the more the "stuff" grows. I believe there's a fine line between letting a child express his personality and letting him junk up a room. Let JAKE help you determine if the furniture and other items in the child's room are appropriate for his age and interests. Ask some questions:

- Is there enough storage space in the room?

- Are the rods in the closet arranged so your child can easily use them?

- Would hooks help your child hang up clothes?

- Is there enough storage space for books, toys, tapes, pictures and items your child creates in school or preschool?

- Are storage bins or crates needed?

- Does your child need a net hung from the wall or ceiling to store stuffed animals?

- Will your child be able to put things away without climbing on a stool? If you want to teach your child to put things away, storage areas must be accessible and easy to use.

JAKE knows if there's a place for everything, it'll be easier for children to put things away. JAKE also knows children must be regularly encouraged to de-junk their rooms. However, by doing this, they'll have rooms that reflect their ages, personalities and interests.

Laundry area

Your laundry area needs a shelf or shelves so you can store all your laundry supplies. It also helps if you have a place to hang clothes that need to dry or that come out of the dryer. If you have room, leave your iron and ironing board set up here. It also makes it easier for children to learn to do the laundry and iron when everything's in one place. Make sure you have a wastebasket handy for lint and fuzz.

Home office

You may have a converted closet or even a separate room for your home office. Regardless of its size, the same principles apply to both a home office and a traditional office. Look for items to eliminate and ways to arrange the space more effectively. And don't let your home office become a handy dumping place for personal items. Treat this space like any other professional office space.

It may be best to have another telephone line installed in your home office. This makes it easier for you to always answer the phone in a professional way. You can also leave a professional message on the answering machine. Buy the best computer equipment you can afford for the work you're doing. Since computer equipment becomes obsolete so quickly, it's best to buy what you need now and plan to upgrade. Other business machines can be purchased used, which saves you money. Always evaluate the price of equipment because you may find it more cost effective to use a business center for specialty jobs, such as copying or faxing.

Storage suggestions

In children's rooms, use colored, plastic bins for storage. The colors make it easy for them to remember where things go. For example, put all the cars in the red bin, books in the blue and tapes in the yellow bin with the tape recorder. A system like this will teach your children to keep their things neat and organized. Remember, it's never too early to learn these skills!

Use clear plastic storage boxes to store out-of-season clothes under the bed. This makes it easy to retrieve things quickly when you need them. Buy cardboard storage boxes (which are sometimes called banker's boxes) to store holiday decorations and other items you use occasionally. There are also special storage containers (both plastic and cardboard) for holiday decorations, but these cost more than the bankers boxes. They can be labeled and stored in the basement, garage or storage shed until you need them. Write directly on the box instead of using labels that can fall off.

Use clear, stackable containers as much as possible so it's easier to find what you need without having to open everything. Use these same suggestions in every area of your personal space to keep clutter under control and still have what you need when you need it.

Summary

When you wage your war on junk at home, it can be harder because many things in your house have sentimental value. So the first step is to decide what's really important to you. Once that's determined, take a look at what isn't being used or what could be eliminated. Attack one room at a time, set a specific time frame and be realistic about what can be done within that time frame.

Usage determines storage, so think about where you store things in your home. Go through each room and ask yourself what storage tools you need to more easily keep things where they belong. Think about your daily routine and the changes that will make your day go more smoothly. Create a list of the things you want to change and then work on bringing more balance and less stress into your life. Don't forget to refer to JAKE's Top Ten as you attack your home space.

Set aside some specific time on your calendar to begin de-junking your personal space. Don't try to do everything at once because this will add to your stress. (Remember baby steps.)

Then create a plan for de-junking your home. Write your plan down here.

JAKE's Top Ten

1. Decide why you're collecting certain items and where you'll display your collection, even before you start to collect.

2. De-junk one room at a time.

3. Make a de-junking appointment and limit it to an hour or less.

4. Usage determines storage at home as well as at work.

5. Clean out storage areas periodically so you'll have more storage space.

6. Clean out your closets and make contributions to a favorite charity.

7. Decide what pieces of furniture, exercise equipment and other unused items need to go.

8. Help your children de-junk their rooms so they'll learn early about having balance in their lives.

9. Don't forget basements, garages, sheds, patios and other areas that need to be de-junked.

10. Packrats and neatniks in the same house will need to compromise.

4 JAKE TACKLES THE PAPER MONSTER AT WORK

A client came to me crying for help because her to-be-filed pile was taller than her five-year-old son. I couldn't wait to see where she kept such an enormous pile. When I went to her office, I immediately saw the problem. She had a pillar with just enough space behind it to hide her filing. She started sticking papers there one day when she wanted to clean up in a hurry before a meeting. The papers fit so well she just kept adding to the pile.

Maybe your to-be-filed pile isn't that bad, but I'm sure you've probably lost a receipt you needed for reimbursement. Perhaps it was a guarantee or warrantee, and you knew it was around somewhere but you just weren't sure where. Or have you ever misplaced a memo from the boss with important deadlines on it?

If you're like most of us, you can identify with at least one of these situations. That's why you need to tackle paper and other information that can junk up your workspace. When you have too much information, it's difficult to find what you really need.

And you may feel like you're drowning in information. The bad news is that information overload isn't going away in the near future. A flood of information continues to flow into your workspace in both paper and electronic forms:

- E-mail

- Voice mail

- Faxes

- Bulk mail

- Telephone solicitations

- Pager messages

- Microfilm or microfiche

- Internet information

- T.V. and radio

- Newspapers

- Magazines

- Reports

This is just a sampling. Regardless of the format, the principles for managing all this information are the same. When de-junking information, keep the following principles in mind.

1. First ask, "Why do I need this information?" We seem to keep a lot of it "just because." When information arrives, think about how you'll actually use it. If you simply ask, "Do I need it?" the answer will almost always be "yes." So be sure to ask "why." If you don't have a specific reason to keep the information, let it go — dump it or delete it.

2. If you decide you need the information, don't keep it any longer than necessary. After you've used it, ask, "Why do I need to keep this information?" If there's another source for retrieving it, let it go. For example, if you're finished using specifications from a vendor and you don't think you'll need them again, throw them out. Later, if you do need them again, contact the vendor. It's the same with that memo from Human Resources. Keep only the things you can't retrieve from another person or place.

3. Don't fall into the trap of being the one in your organization who hangs on to everything. One woman told me she was afraid to throw things away because co-workers depended on her to keep everything. She even kept things other people created. I asked her, "If the originator didn't think it was important enough to keep, why do you think it's so important?" "Just in case" and "just because" are two of the worst reasons in the world. Be sure you have a valid business reason for keeping information — not just a feeling you may need it someday.

Make a list in the space below of all the types of information you receive regularly. Then indicate which ones you eliminate and make a plan to do so.

JAKE uses RAFT

JAKE knows that when information starts floating across your desk — whether it's electronic or paper — there are only four things you can do with it. Just remember RAFT if you feel like you're drowning in information.

- R stands for refer. Often items arrive on your desk that should really go to someone else. Don't let them stay on your desk. Forward them as quickly as possible. In fact, have a specific place to put them so they don't clutter up your workspace. If you regularly receive items you don't need or use, have your name taken off the distribution list.

- A stands for action. Although time-management experts tell you to handle each piece of paper only once, studies show that items are usually handled about eight to 10 times. Even if you reduce this to four or five times you're de-junking your life. Put action items in a specific place until you're ready to work on them. A tickler file, which I'll explain in Chapter 6, is a great way to keep these items organized.

- F stands for filing. This is for items you'll need for future reference. A wonderful filing tool is a sorter. There are different types of sorters that will help you keep your filing from becoming a pile. Use a vertical sorter so it's easy to retrieve information without digging through a pile of paper. Sorters may be expandable file folders, books with expandable binding and plastic, or metal or wheel types. Check an office supply store for different kinds of sorters and choose the one that best fits the way you handle paper.

- T stands for toss, which includes recycling. Don't let things accumulate. Get rid of them immediately by keeping those wastebaskets and recycling bins within easy reach.

Filing

Let's look at filing in more detail since this is one of the best ways to keep information under control. When you file, there are several things to consider. First think about how you want to keep the information. Are you going to keep it on paper or on your computer? In most cases, avoid storing the information in both formats. If you have a good back-up procedure, you should feel comfortable about keeping your information on computer files.

Another consideration is how long you should keep filed items. Your organization should have a retention schedule that tells you what documents to keep and for how long. There are legal requirements for the retention schedule. For items that aren't listed on a retention schedule, use your common sense. Periodically clean out your files and toss what you don't need anymore. You might do this three or four times a year.

Six ways to file

Tame your paper monster by remembering items can only be filed using one of six methods.

1. One way of filing is by subject. While subject files are very common, they can be difficult to use if you forget how you filed the item. For example, say you're working with information about lions and tigers. When you put it away, you placed it in a file labeled "felines." A couple of days later you tried to find the information and looked for a file "lions." Not there. You looked under "tigers" and then "cats." Not there either. You asked a co-worker and she suggested looking under "animals" or "fuzzy." Still no luck. So always consider how you're going to use the information. In this example, you should have filed it under "predators" since that's your project title.

2. Another way to file information is by priority or in order of importance. Files are arranged with the most important one first, the second most important next and so on. This system can help you keep up with your most important projects.

3. In alphabetical files, information is classified and filed alphabetically. This system's very popular for working files. For instance, you might have a file for a client whose name begins with "a" in the same alphabetical category as a project file that also starts with "a."

4. When information is filed by date this is called chronological filing. Some examples of chronological filing would be filing a letter or invoice by the date it was created.

5. Numerical files are best used for items that you want to keep confidential or for items that already have numbers assigned to them, such as purchase orders or invoices. If you create numerical files for confidentially, you'll also need an alphabetical listing of all your numerical files so you can always locate them. For example, instead of filing client files by name, there would be a number assigned to that file and that's where it would go in the system. The numbers may be assigned sequentially (in order the files are created), or numbers may be designated for each letter of the alphabet and a number is assigned using the numerical equivalent of the client's name. Numbers may also be assigned by categories. Since this is a time-consuming system to use, try to avoid it unless absolutely necessary.

6. The last possibility for classifying information is by location or geography. This can be as small as an area in a building or as large as a city, state or country. An example of geographical filing is arranging your client files by the cities in which they're located. This makes it easy to gather all of your client files when you're visiting them in that city.

This is the good news — there are only six ways to classify information! When you set up your files, consider having several small filing systems that match the usage of the information. I have my client files in an alphabetical system by client or company name. I have all my training programs filed by subject because that's how I use this information. My invoices are in a numerical file by invoice number so they're easy to track. This is more productive than having one system and trying to force everything to fit into it. Multiple systems can make filing and retrieving information much easier. Always ask yourself, "How will this information be used?" and let that guide how you file it.

Tackling the big stacks

If you have a huge to-be-filed pile, it may seem overwhelming to even get started. Ignore the big stack and instead concentrate on your current information using your RAFT and a sorter. Set time aside each day to stay up-to-date with your filing for at least three weeks. After you've kept on top of it that long, you can start attacking your backlogged filing. Take only a few items at a time from the stack and incorporate them into your current filing process. Even if it takes you 18 months to get through your to-be-filed pile, you're making progress. The good news is, as you work your way down the stack, you'll be able to throw away a lot of old, outdated information.

Usage determines storage

You'll recall that "usage determines storage" is a great tip for de-junking and balancing your life. This is true for information as well as space. The more you use something, the closer it should be to you. Your personal working files should be close to your desk or in your desk drawers. Any files you use on a regular basis, but not daily, can be stored in file cabinets in or near your office.

Piles of information on your desk can interfere with your productivity because they take up valuable desk space. If you need this information at your fingertips, use vertical file holders to store them on the outer edge of your desk or a close shelf. Since you don't have to dig through piles, this makes it much faster and easier to find a particular file or piece of information.

Another consideration when de-junking your life is where you file information. If you're not careful, a filing cabinet can also double as another place to stack and pile information. If you use a filing cabinet, keep a vertical file holder on top to eliminate possible piles.

Look at the tools you currently use to keep information under control. What works? What doesn't work? What do you need to be more effective in managing information?

Reflections

Sticky notes

Beware of sticky notes because they can sometimes fall off or travel to places you never intended them to go. They also look unprofessional if you have faded old notes stuck around the edges of your computer screen or on your wall. Only use sticky notes for temporary bits of information. Better yet, try the note posting feature on your computer, which keeps those little snippets of information on the edges of documents. Like traditional sticky notes, they can quickly be deleted when you no longer need them.

A filing appointment

Dennis was a client of mine in Washington state who had to deal with regulations concerning hazardous waste disposal. His secretary would file the regulations in binders, and then he would try to scan them once a week. Because he was always behind in reading the regulations he made a plan. He decided to take the first five minutes of each day to scan the regulations and put them in binders himself. At the end of the day he would take five more minutes to scan and file the regulations. This method allowed him to stay current. Regardless of how busy the day might be, he could always spare at least five minutes before starting other work each morning. It also helped that co-workers were willing to leave him alone for five minutes, which didn't seem like a very long time.

By using a sorter, your papers are somewhat organized ahead of time so they're easier to file. Think of a sorter as a temporary holding place for your papers until you have time to file them. Set an appointment to file once or twice a week so you can stay up to date. If you have a great deal of filing, you might need to do it on a daily basis. If there's less to file, once or twice a month may be enough. Remember that it's up to you to decide the best way to de-junk your life.

If you have backlogged filing, ignore it for now and concentrate on keeping up with current information. Make a plan for dealing with this backlog three months from today.

Reflections

Computer files

Follow the same principles that govern paper files to control your computer files. Think "usage determines storage" — how you use the information determines how it should be filed. Another key to de-junking is to match the categories of your paper files and your computer files. If these are the same, you'll be able to find things more easily.

Use your computer directories and subdirectories like the primary and secondary categories in your paper files. Don't keep more than three levels of either computer or paper files. For example, the primary heading might be "Maintenance," with "Streets" as a secondary heading. Then you might have subfiles named "Light" and "Signs." This keeps the systems simple and easy to use.

Naming your computer files also can be a challenge. Simplicity is the key. Talk to your co-workers about naming files and be consistent in choosing names. Also arrange your computer files by usage, with the most often-used files first in your directories or subdirectories.

Newspapers

Newspapers and newsletters that you subscribe to for professional reasons can be overwhelming. Read the newspapers immediately or at least go through them for articles you might need later. Cut the articles out, date them and then place them in a newspaper reading file. The rule for this file should be that articles can only stay in the file for one week. If you haven't read the article within the week, then throw it away. If you have trouble throwing these away, enlist a clutter buddy to do it for you.

Magazines

Magazines are another prime way to junk up your life. I subscribe to several with the idea that I'll keep some of them. For the magazines I don't keep, I cut out the articles I want and recycle the rest of the magazine. Then I date those articles and put them in a magazine reading folder. The rule for this folder is that articles can only stay for 30 days. After 30 days I discard them.

Some magazines and trade journals I keep as a resource for two years. First I make a photocopy of the index and then place it in a binder with other index copies for that same magazine. The magazine then goes on a shelf in another area. When I need to look for a particular article, it's much easier to grab the binder and look through the indexes until I find what I need. Then I go to the shelf for the resource itself.

The library is a great source for magazines and newspapers you need occasionally. So is the Internet. You can read an article at your leisure and then print a copy if you need it for research or a specific use. Later, if you need it again, you can search the Internet again. This saves both paper and time. So be ruthless about getting rid of newspapers and magazines you don't need or have time to read.

Other types of information

Voice mail and pagers are great tools because it's difficult to make a paper copy of the information you receive. This forces you to deal with it immediately and then move on to other things. I believe it's important to respond to messages quickly so you don't have a backlog to handle.

However, faxes and e-mail can junk up your life because they're so easy for people to send. One friend received more than 60 e-mail messages in just one weekend. Talk about information overload! He didn't want any of the messages, but unfortunately he had to take the time to handle them anyway. Be ruthless in dealing with information regardless of how it arrives.

Eliminate unwanted contacts

If you receive lots of bulk mail that you don't want, contact the Direct Marketing Association's Customer Service Division by calling (202) 955-5030. A representative will tell you how to have your name removed from bulk-mail lists. Check the Consumer Information section of your phone book for the telephone number to call to reduce telephone solicitations. Advertisers don't want to spend their advertising dollars on people who aren't interested in their products or services, so it's a win-win situation for everyone. JAKE definitely recommends you take control of unwanted information by getting your name and phone number removed from these lists.

Summary

You need a plan to handle your information overload, and the first step is deciding why you really need to keep something. Stay afloat by using your RAFT when information crosses your desk. Since there are only six ways to file information, decide which system or systems you want to use and get a sorter to keep your filing organized all the time. Follow the same principles that govern paper files to keep your computer files under control. Simplicity is the key when dealing with information, whether it's electronic or paper. Use whatever tools you can to stop or slow down unsolicited information. Now here's JAKE with his Top ten.

JAKE's Top Ten

1. Remember, as always, usage determines storage.

2. Let directories and subdirectories help keep computer files under control.

3. Be consistent about how you name and use both your computer files and paper files.

4. Beware of how you use sticky notes.

5. Use the Internet as a resource for current information.

6. Find a clutter buddy to help you throw things away.

7. Use your RAFT to stay afloat in the information age.

8. Eliminate your to-be-filed pile by using a sorter.

9. Make a filing appointment with yourself and then do it on a regular basis.

10. Remember "Horizontal it's a pile, vertical it's a file." Use vertical file holders to get rid of your stacks and piles of paper.

5 JAKE HITS THE HOME PAPER PILES

Anne, a successful, well-dressed young woman told me she had a problem paying her bills. It wasn't lack of money, she just didn't have time to pay them. It would take her hours to get the bills ready, write the checks, keep track of them in her checkbook register and then mail them.

Her method of handling bills was to throw them all in a shoebox each day when she got home from work. When she had time, she would sort through the entire shoebox, pay what was due and leave the rest until next time. The reason she had problems paying her bills was because she didn't have a plan to handle them effectively. This is just one area of your personal life that JAKE can help you de-junk.

Information piles up in your personal life as well as your professional life. Think about all the "junk" that accumulates at home:

- Junk mail
- Sale fliers
- Informational fliers
- Catalogs
- Brochures
- Newspapers
- Magazines

- Books
- Videos
- Audio tapes
- CDs
- Photographs
- Mementos
- Personal business papers

The list seems endless. Therefore, you need a plan to control the personal information that floods into your home. Since some of it's very important, you need to keep it well organized and easily accessible. However, a lot isn't important to you at all and needs to be tossed immediately. Then there are things that fall in-between these two categories. Whatever the case, rely on JAKE to help you deal with information overload.

Junk mail

This is one thing everyone has to handle. Start by deciding what's really important to you. If you don't have an interest in gardening, get your name off the gardening supplies mailing list. Create a form letter to contact companies like these to let them know you have no interest in their products or services. They won't want to waste their mailing dollars on people like you who won't buy anything. If you think that someday you might be interested in their products or services, you can always call and they'll be glad to start sending you information again.

If your name is on several mailing lists and you don't have any interest in these companies, you can contact the Direct Marketing Association's Customer Services Division at (202) 955-5030 to have your name removed. When you do order something, tell the company you don't want your name sold or given to any other organizations, even if the products or services are the same or similar.

I use certain arrangements of the letters of my first name and middle initial when I purchase something by phone or on the Internet. I also do the same thing when I join associations or organizations. If my name shows up on a new mailing list, I know who violated my request not to sell or give my name out. I then deal directly with that organization.

Sale papers, catalogs, brochures and fliers

Since these are all date sensitive, keep them only if you're interested in what's being offered. Determine this the day you receive them. As soon as they're outdated get rid of them. If the brochures and fliers are for activities, record the information on your calendar and toss them immediately.

Catalogs should only be kept if you are serious about ordering something. If you recycle the catalog and decide later that you want to order a product, be sure you know how to contact the company. In fact, you may want to keep a list of 800 numbers for the catalog companies you're interested in using. In most cases these companies can take care of your needs even if you don't have their catalogs.

It can be very challenging to keep up with all these catalogs because they change frequently. If you don't have the most current issue, what you want may not be in stock, the price may be different or some other change may have taken place.

The Internet

The Internet is a wonderful place to find information. You have almost unlimited resources, especially for current information, and you can print a hard copy if you need it. If you don't need a hard copy, the information is still at your fingertips and ready to use. To avoid wasting paper, don't print anything unless you absolutely have to.

List the subscriptions you currently receive. Do you really need each one? Are they really worth the time and energy it takes to control all the information? Which ones can you cancel now? Make a plan to cancel the ones you don't read.

Reflections

Videos, audio tapes and CDs

Videos, audio tapes and CDs offer their own special challenge because you may add to your collection frequently. Be sure to set aside a place to store these items. You might arrange them in the following ways:

Store movies alphabetically by their names since this is how you probably look for them. (Usage determines storage.)

Tapes may be arranged by topic or alphabetically. If you have music tapes, you might arrange them by type of music or by artist. Arrange your motivational and learning tapes by topic or the name of the presenter, if that's how you would look for them. (Again, usage determines storage.)

Keep CDs arranged by type and usage too. You may have software CDs that should be kept near your computer. Music CDs should be stored the same way you store music tapes.

Be consistent in how you store these items so it's easy for everyone in the family to find and use them. When you're organizing movies, tapes and CDs, weed out the ones you don't want or need any longer. These make great garage-sale items.

Books

Books present their own special challenge for me. Because I love to read, and I live in a house full of people who also love to read, we have a constant influx of books covering a wide variety of subjects in both fiction and nonfiction. We read both paperback and hardback books, and they accumulate at an alarming rate.

As a result, we divide them into two types of books: the "keeper" and the "lender or give-away" book. We place the lender or give-away books in one of two locations. Everyone in the family knows if a book's in one of those spots, it's available to loan or give away to anyone who wants it. A "keeper" book is one we've decided is important enough to keep. It can be loaned out, but only after checking with the owner first. One of our lender section's located in the guestroom, and the other is in the hall, making it easy and quick to locate a lender or give-away book. Even with this plan, we still have problems with our books not always being in the right spot.

For nonfiction books, I arrange them by type of book since that's the way I generally use their information. The fiction books are arranged by the author's name. Computer books are located on a shelf above the computer for quick reference. In this case usage determines storage.

Go through all your books, videotapes, audiotapes and CDs and organize them in a way that fits your lifestyle. Then gather all those you don't want or use anymore and donate them to a charity or sell them in a garage sale. Write the date you plan to do this here.

Reflections

Mementos and photographs

Some items in your home are very important to you, such as mementos and photographs. Of course, some are more important than others. I remember my parents always took lots of pictures of scenery and then couldn't remember where the picture was taken. These pictures should have been thrown away. Instead, they provided food for "discussion" every time we looked at them so they actually junked up our lives in more than one way.

When deciding how to store photographs, think about how much time you have to invest in caring for them. I have a family member who has photograph albums arranged by year. Each picture is labeled with a little information about what's happening in it. Another family member keeps all her photographs in photo storage boxes labeled by year.

Only you can decide what works best for your pictures. If you're a right-brain person, don't add stress and frustration to your life by deciding to create photo albums with decorations, cutouts, clever captions and other time-consuming details. You probably won't be able to keep up with it, making it something else you don't have time for. De-junk your life by spending time and energy on the things that are really important to you.

Mementos from trips are the same way. At the time they seem so great, but in a few years they may have no meaning to you. At that point, it's time to let the happy warrior JAKE go to battle and get rid of them. Don't let items that no longer have personal meaning for you junk up your life.

Children's mementos

Those of you with children have to get serious about weeding out all the treasures your child brings home from preschool and school. One of my clients has a box for each of her children. The items they bring home are placed in the box after they've been displayed for awhile. When the box is full, a memento has to be thrown away before another one is put in the box. This way she controls the number of mementos her children collect. What a great way to save only the best of all those childhood treasures! If you don't stay on top of them, they'll become overwhelming.

Personal business papers

People de-junk their lives to achieve balance, reduce stress and focus on what's really important to them. One area that needs to be under control is your personal business papers. Bills to be paid, receipts, warrantees and income tax information are all vital documents that need to be well-organized. This prevents documents from being lost, bills from not being paid, warrantees from not being available when they're needed and other frustrating experiences.

If it's necessary to move these important papers around frequently, you might keep them in a file crate. If you don't have an office or desk at home, keep the crate in your closet and carry it to a table when it's time to take care of your personal business. When you're finished, put the crate put away until it's needed again. Make sure each file's clearly marked.

Have plan in place

Remember Anne, the young woman I mentioned at the beginning of the chapter? She needed a plan for her bills. Since she didn't have a desk at home, I recommended she buy a small holder with hanging files. I helped her set up a system to pay her bills on the fifth and 20th of each month. She made a folder for the fifth and another one for the 20th and she simply drops her bills in the correct folder so they're easy to find when it's time to pay them. Then she schedules an appointment on those two days to actually pay her bills. She's also established a simple tickler file to remind her when it's time to pay her bills.

I also recommended Anne use a computer program to keep her financial information current. The program writes her checks, deducts the amount from her check register and makes it easy for her to balance her bank statements — something she hadn't done in several years.

Now Anne's able to meet her financial obligations without the task taking hours to complete. She also created a file for receipts and another one for warrantees. She feels more successful and less stressed because she has a place to store these things and a plan to follow through on handling them. It only took a little time and effort to get her finances under control. A plan like this pays big dividends in how Anne feels about herself and how it de-junks her life.

Vital documents

Some papers are so important that they need to be protected by being placed, in a safety-deposit box, at your attorney or CPA's office or in some other safe location. These vital documents include anything you would need to keep functioning in case of a disaster. After talking with people who lived through the Northridge, Calif., earthquake, the one theme repeated numerous times was, "I didn't know who my insurance agent was, and I couldn't find my important papers. What a mess!"

What vital documents do you need to protect? Make a list and decide where you will keep these important papers. It would be wise to store one list in a safety-deposit box and another list with a relative or friend.

Summary

Use JAKE to keep information under control at home. You need a plan to control all the types of information you have there. When you have a place for everything — from mementos to videos and CDs — you'll have less stress in your life. You'll also have more time to spend doing things with family and friends. Here's JAKE's Top Ten to help you attack the information overload at home.

JAKE's Top Ten

1. Have a plan for your personal business papers and information and then use it.

2. Store vital documents in a safe location.

3. Be consistent in the way you store videos, movies, audio tapes and CDs.

4. Be selective about magazine subscriptions.

5. Use alternative sources for information, such as the Internet and libraries.

6. Write an activity's date and information on your calendar and then toss the original announcement.

7. Don't subscribe to a newspaper unless you read it consistently. Consider having only a weekend subscription.

8. If you keep catalogs, store them together in one place and replace old copies when the new ones arrive.

9. Limit the number of mementos you save.

10. Contact the Direct Marketing Association to remove your name from junk-mail lists.

6 JAKE MAKES TIME AT WORK

It was early one morning when the pastor leisurely got out of bed. Since he was the only one awake, he grabbed a cup of coffee and sat on the patio enjoying the quiet moment. Suddenly the idea hit him — "I'll go fishing!" He jumped up, quickly grabbed his fishing gear, left a note for his wife and headed for the lake. After a wonderful time fishing, he headed for home a little after noon. His wife greeted him at the door in a state of panic. "Did you forget about the wedding you were supposed to perform at 10 this morning?"

Maybe you haven't forgotten something as important as a wedding, but most of us can identify with a missed appointment or a forgotten deadline. Managing time is a problem for most people. Since you only have 24 hours in each day, it's vital to use the time you have wisely and effectively.

If you want to de-junk your life, you need time on your side in order to win the war. I believe it's a matter of self-management that allows you to stay balanced, focused and able to accomplish your necessary and important tasks all while using time effectively. The pastor who forgot the wedding had it written down on his calendar, but he just forgot to check it. He didn't use good self-management skills.

Ben Franklin once said, "Dost thou love life? Then do not squander time, for that is the stuff life is made of." Most of you think, "I wish I had more time," or "If I only had more time I could do something I really enjoy." When you start de-junking your life by being better organized, putting your energy into things that matter to you and being realistic about what's possible to accomplish, you'll have balance, less stress and more time to do things you enjoy. JAKE can help you win the war with time.

Self-management

De-junking your time is a difficult task. However, it pays great dividends when you're able to spend more time doing what's important to you and less time doing things that don't provide the rewards you want. Don't think of it as time management — think of it as self-management. This reminds you that you're responsible for managing yourself to get the best results from the time you're investing. In order to achieve effective self-management, you need some tools for de-junking your time.

Start with a calendar

A basic tool for self-management is a calendar since it provides a written record of how you're spending time. Take charge of your time and de-junk your life of activities and commitments you don't want to be involved in. It requires discipline to schedule your time effectively and deliberately, but it also helps balance your life and reduce your stress. Ask yourself, "Why am I involved in this activity?" If there isn't a compelling reason, let go of the activity. You change and circumstances change, so let go of activities that aren't important to you anymore.

You'll never be able to take charge of your time effectively if you don't use a calendar consistently. I have clients who tell me they plan their day in their heads so they don't need to write things down. They also confess they lose information, forget appointments and spend valuable time trying to find addresses and phone numbers that could be right at their fingertips if they used a calendar.

Your calendar is much more than a diagram of the 12 months of the year, whether it's on paper or in your computer. A good calendar system should have the following sections:

- Day-by-day display

- Monthly overview

- Place for your to-do list

- Expense record section

- Address section

- Place for diary information or notes

Some of you may need a yearly overview section if you block out large segments of time for conferences, training events or other activities. If you're constantly adding little notes, losing information and missing appointments, your calendar may be too small, so consider one with more space for recording items.

At the same time, use the simplest calendar possible. If your current calendar doesn't meet your needs, then buy another one. Even if it's the middle of the year, the money you invest in a new calendar system will pay for itself in effectiveness and time saved. If you find your calendar frustrating to use, you'll soon stop using it. That can lead to disaster when you're trying to de-junk your life.

You should use one calendar for both professional and personal information, and it should be portable if you're constantly on the go. If your secretary keeps a calendar for you and you keep one too, make sure anytime an entry is made in one calendar, it's also placed on the other one immediately. If you violate this rule, you'll find yourself missing an important appointment or making appointments to be in two places at the same time. To really de-junk and achieve balance in your life, you need a specific procedure for handling duplicate calendars.

Most of you probably need a calendar that's portable. If you're using a computer-based program, take a paper copy of your daily and monthly calendar with you when you leave the office. That way you'll always know what's next on your schedule, and you'll also be able to set up future appointments. When you return to the office immediately enter any changes or additions to your computer calendar. There are several computer software packages available that are similar to paper calendars. Talk to a software salesperson about the kind of paper system you like best. This can help you select the software package that would work best for you.

Computer-based calendars have some wonderful features to help you stay on track. They can do some or all of the following:

- Carry "to do" items from one day to the next (my favorite feature)

- Sound alarms to remind you of appointments

- Include search capabilities that help you look for specific information

- Make it easy to reschedule appointments

- Provide time log and summary of time use

- Allow an assistant or associate to schedule things even if you're away from your workplace

- Warn you about overlapping appointments

JAKE and a PDA

Another useful device is a handheld PDA (personal digital assistant). These tools offer much more than a calendar. They can keep your calendar, names and phone numbers, memo functions and reminders of birthdays and anniversaries. Some PDAs also have word processing and money management programs, modems and e-mail capabilities. When considering a PDA, be sure it's compatible with your computer to easily transfer information from one device to another. I recently watched a salesman access his e-mail, handle 60 messages quickly, download a file to his computer and enter three new appointments, all using the modem in his PDA. He did all this while he was on his lunch hour. A PDA is a wonderful time-saver for people on the move.

More than just a calendar

Use your calendar to keep up with different types of information. When you make an appointment with someone, write in your calendar the telephone number, address and directions to where you will meet that person on that particular date. This saves time and energy when it's time to actually go to the meeting. You only have one place to look for the information you need.

I have one client who constantly writes down information, however, he often forgets where he wrote it down. One time he'll write the information on the day he makes the appointment, and the next time he'll write it on the date of the appointment. You need a consistent method when recording information for appointments and other commitments. That way you're not constantly searching in different places for your information.

Your calendar also can provide one place to record all of the following:

- Information about conversations you have with other people

- Tasks you've delegated to someone else

- A diary section where you can record the contributions you make to your organization

- A tabbed address section that can double as a filing place for items you need at your fingertips when you're out of the office

- A place to write ideas, thoughts, suggestions and plans for the future

- A place to record goals you've set for yourself as well as action plans to accomplish those goals

Talk to productive people you admire about the types of calendars they use. This can give you suggestions and ideas to help you select the best calendar for your needs. Remember your left-brain/right-brain tendencies when selecting a calendar. If you're a right-brain person and the calendar is too detailed, it may be hard for you to use effectively. If you're a left-brain person, you'll probably be very comfortable with a detailed calendar. Don't try to make your calendar fit you — find one that works with your natural tendencies, not against them. Your calendar should help you, not frustrate you. Remember one size does not fit all. However, the simpler your system, the more likely you are to use it.

Evaluate your current calendar. Is it the best one for you? Do you need to make changes in the way you record appointments? Remember to use the simplest calendar possible. List all of the things you now keep in your calendar. What should you add to help you better control your time?

Reflections

Your most important appointment

Regardless of the type of calendar you use, make an appointment with yourself each day to plan your time. If you give yourself the gift of just 10 minutes a day, it can pay large dividends. You'll have an opportunity to look at the day, week and even the month so you can be proactive rather than reactive. When you're proactive, you get the best results because you've planned what, when, where, how and why you should spend time on something. Being proactive also makes it easier for you to work effectively with other people. It helps you balance, control and de-junk your life.

It's estimated that for every one minute you spend planning, you save three minutes in doing a task. Add a daily planning appointment to your calendar and don't let anything short of a real emergency cancel this appointment. When you see how much you'll be able to accomplish by using those 10 to 15 golden minutes each day, you'll wonder why it took you so long to make an appointment with yourself. Your calendar is your best tool for staying on track and for de-junking and balancing your life.

Controllable time

When you're planning your day, schedule time for yourself. You should schedule at least an hour a day to work on things important to you but not urgent. I call this controllable or discretionary time. This should be quiet, uninterrupted time that allows you to concentrate and focus on important tasks. Be consistent about taking the time to plan and work on these projects. Controllable time helps you keep your life balanced and free of junk.

Making a master list

A master list of the major projects you want to accomplish also helps you use your time wisely. This includes tasks relating to both long-term and short-term projects. When you have a master list it's easier to see the big picture, to get an overview of what's ahead. Use your master list to write down ideas relating to your projects. This will help you decide what should be included on your daily to-do list.

The master list eliminates little pieces of paper and small lists that are easily lost. Your master list should have the date of your entry on the left side of the page and the due date on the right side of the page. This helps you decide on a daily basis how to spend your time wisely and still complete your projects. If you write your master list by hand, use pencil so you can make changes. I keep my master list on the computer and just print it out when I need a hard copy. This makes it easy to make changes and keep my list current.

To-do list

Another self-management tool is a daily to-do list. You record everything you want or need to do in the course of one day on your to-do list. It should take you about 10 minutes. If it takes longer, then you probably have too much on it. Once again, I like to create mine on the computer since it's so much faster for me than writing it by hand. This also makes it easier to transfer any items I didn't complete to the next day's list.

You can write your to-do list first thing in the morning to plan for that day. Or at the end of the day you can write your to-do list for the next day. This again depends on how you work most effectively. Since I have the kind of mind that best processes information at night, I write my to-do list at the end of the previous day.

When you create your to-do list, carry over any tasks left undone from the day before. Then review your master list and select the tasks that need to be taken care of that day. Be realistic about what you can actually accomplish. If you have lots of meetings, you'll probably have time for only smaller tasks. If your day has a large block of unscheduled time, then it's a great day to tackle a bigger project.

Don't expect to get it all done all the time

Realize you won't finish everything on your to-do list every single day. Some days you'll complete the entire list and have time left over, but most of the time you'll have more tasks than time.

After you've created your to-do list, decide which are the three most important tasks of the day and get started on them. After they're done, pick the next three tasks to be completed. Work your way through your to-do list by staying focused on the tasks you decide are the most important ones on the list. This de-junks your time of things that aren't productive or that don't accomplish the goals you've set for the day.

Are you using a to do-list effectively or are you overestimating what you think you can accomplish each day? Remember, your to-do list should only take about ten minutes to write. Use the space below to write a sample to-do list for a typical day at work. Try to be realistic about your accomplishments.

Reflections

Tickler file

A tickler file is one of my favorite de-junking tools because it gives me a place to put things until I need them. I don't have to remember where I put something because it will always be in the tickler file. It allows me to use my time more effectively because I'm not wasting time looking for things in several different places.

My tickler file has 43 folders that I keep in a large desk drawer. There are 31 daily folders labeled one through 31 for each day of the month. The labels on the other 12 folders have the months of the year on them. The first folder in the drawer is for the current month. Following this monthly folder are the daily folders. Behind folder 31 is the folder for the next month, along with the daily folders for all those days that have already past in the current month.

For instance, if today's date were May 19, my tickler file would have May as the first folder followed by the daily folders numbered 19 through 31. Behind folder 31 would be June's monthly folder and then the daily folders numbered one through 18. Next would come the monthly folders for July through April.

At the end of the day, I would check folder 19 to make sure all the items had been handled or assigned another date. Then I would put folder 19 behind folder 18 for June. Essentially I'm creating a daily file for the next 31 days. A tickler file like this also ensures that I have a place to put items I need to deal with in the months to come.

I use my tickler file to keep up with anything that is paper-based. For example, today I received an airplane ticket I won't use until July, so I dropped it in the July folder. I also called several people today and I'm waiting for some of them to call me back. I drop their telephone slips in the daily folder for a couple of days from now. When I check that folder, I'll be reminded that I need to call these people if I haven't heard from them yet.

There's one disadvantage to a tickler file: You must be disciplined and check it every single day. At the end of the day, when I'm checking the current daily folder to make sure everything's been taken care of, I'll also check the folder for the next day. This gives me an opportunity to plan for tomorrow so I'm not surprised by what I might find in my tickler file when I come to work the next day. If you don't check the night before, you must check your tickler file as soon as you get to work. If you don't, you might get busy and forget an important appointment or deadline.

A simpler tickler file might work better for you. Some people just use daily folders because they don't have a lot of activity more than 31 days in advance. You also may prefer to use a small box and slips of paper or cards to remind you of the things you need to do. Maybe you only need a tickler file with five folders, one for each day of the week. It simply depends on how many items you need to keep track of on a daily basis. Play around with the tickler file concept to find what works best for you.

Think about how you might benefit from using a tickler file. What type of tickler file would be best for you? Do you need folders to store information or can you use a computerized tickler file? Make plans about to set up a tickler file as soon as possible.

Reflections

Reflections

Peak productivity time

You'll be able to accomplish more if you're aware of your peak productivity times and then schedule your day with these times in mind. Your peak productivity times are those when you're working at your very best. Most people have several periods of time during the day when they're able to accomplish a lot of work with very little effort.

Determine your peak productivity times by keeping a log of how you spend your time for a week. Start in the middle of the week because Mondays can be very hectic, which might make it tempting to postpone keeping the time log. Fridays also can be busy because you're getting ready for the weekend and you might have last-minute projects to finish.

To find your peak productivity time, record your activities on a time-log sheet. I prefer a time-log sheet with two-hour increments to record my energy levels. For eight to 10 days, identify your energy level as high, medium or low and then evaluate the pattern you see. The high-energy times reflect your peak productivity, when you'll be able to handle difficult tasks more effectively.

When you have complicated tasks to do and it's not your peak productivity time, be realistic and allow extra time for the work. Also when you're in a non-peak productivity time, you're more likely to make mistakes so allow time to check and recheck your work. Better yet, try to use your less productive time for routine tasks that don't take much concentration or those that allow you to move around. This can be a good time for making copies, sending faxes, taking a coffee break and spending some time away from your work area.

Time-saving technology

Faxes, e-mail, voice mail, telephones, cell phones, pagers, networked computer systems, modems and scanners are just some of the tools that help you do your work more effectively and with less effort. However, they can also junk up your life by making you constantly accessible to other people who expect information and answers from you immediately.

Group your tasks together to use time and technology more effectively. Send faxes at 10:30 a.m. and 3:30 p.m. instead of running to the fax machine every time someone needs a fax sent. Check your e-mail and voice mail at specific times: first thing in the morning, just after lunch and right before you leave at night. Use either e-mail or voice mail systems to distribute information quickly to a large number of people.

Voice mail is a wonderful tool because it frees us from time differences. I even use voice mail to leave myself messages. If I wake up in the middle of the night with a great idea or the solution to a problem, I leave myself a message on my voice mail. That's much easier than turning on the light, finding a pencil and paper and writing it down.

Many people don't like voice mail because it's often not used correctly. Be sure to keep your voice mail message current. If you're out of the office all day, leave that information on your message so people won't expect you to call them back within an hour. Leave the times when you'll be returning calls so people know when to expect your call. This cuts down on telephone tag and allows both you and other people to use time more effectively.

Voice mail messages should be as short as possible. One of the first things the caller should hear is how to skip the message. It's time consuming and irritating to have to listen to a long message with nine options. Limit the options to three or less and keep your message short and simple. If possible, tell callers how to reach another person in case of emergency.

Summary

Time is a valuable commodity, so you need to have effective self-management skills to make the most of your time. Some basic tools to help you spend your time wisely are a calendar, master list and to-do list. Also, look to technology — such as voice mail — to help you manage yourself more effectively. Remember your left-brain/right-brain tendencies when selecting your self-management tools so you're working with your strengths, not against them. Also check out JAKE's Top Ten for de-junking your time.

JAKE's Top Ten

1. Make an appointment with yourself the most important appointment of the day and keep it consistently.

2. Find the calendar that works best for you. Don't hesitate to change calendars if the one you're currently using isn't effective.

3. Create checklists for activities or projects that will be repeated.

4. Group like tasks together. Make all your telephone calls just before lunch or at the end of the day. Most people are at their desks then and they're willing to handle business quickly because they're eager to go to lunch or leave for the day.

5. Create a master list and a to-do list to use your time more effectively. However, don't have too many lists because they'll get lost or become confusing.

6. Learn how to use your computer's full capabilities. It's estimated that most of us only use about 20 percent of them.

7. Invest in technology that'll help you achieve your goals. Don't get a gadget just because it seems like the "in" thing to have. Know how it will benefit you.

8. Create a tickler file to keep information about upcoming projects, deadlines, meetings and activities. Make it simple to use.

9. Know your peak productivity time and use it to do your most difficult projects whenever possible.

10. De-junking and balancing your life is a self-management issue.

7 JAKE MAKES TIME AT HOME

Do you have enough time to do the things you really want to do? Do you wish you had more time to take care of yourself? Are you trying to find more time to spend with your family? Are you looking for ways to cut down on your chores at home? Then read on because JAKE has some great tips for you to use in managing your time at home.

My friends Bob and Shelly have three children, two cats and a dog. Bob's job takes him out of town frequently, and Shelly works part-time out of their home. Their four-year-old hasn't started school yet, but she has playgroup three days a week, and soccer, gymnastics and dance lessons each week. The two elementary-age kids are involved in music lessons, church activities and sports, including soccer, basketball and baseball. Bob and Shelly are also very active in their church. Once Shelly confided to me that she felt like she was losing her mind with everyone in the family going in different directions all the time. She said, "I feel like my life is out of balance, and there's something wrong here! Life shouldn't be one big race from early morning until late at night."

Like Shelly, most of you are looking for balance in your lives. Time seems to be one area that gets out of balance very quickly. Your first conflict involving time may be between your professional and personal responsibilities. When you get home from work you have lots of choices about how to spend your time. Here are just a few:

- Social activities

- Church and school activities

- Recreational activities

- Exercise or health-related activities

- Civic activities

- Household chores

- Yard work

- Reading or watching TV

These are all worthwhile and important, however, most of you don't have enough time for all of them. This is why you need to use your self-management skills when making decisions about how to spend your personal time.

The family calendar

Even in your personal life, the calendar is a basic tool. If you have one family calendar with all activities recorded on it, any family member can tell at a glance what's happening. This calendar should be in a central location, such as the kitchen. Try using a different color for each person so it's even easier to see what everyone's doing at any given time. With a family calendar, you can easily see when you're over-committed and then begin to take steps to balance your activities. A family calendar also shows you if you're spending enough time together as a family. It's easier to evaluate your personal time when everything's written down.

Keeping up with everyone and everything

Sit down at the beginning of the year and record important dates on your central household calendar — birthdays, anniversaries, holidays and planned vacations. This helps everyone remember these dates and prevents someone from planning something else on a special day, such as going fishing with buddies on an anniversary or birthday. A good calendar can help reduce friction among household members.

Make sure the central calendar includes time for extended family and close friends to be together. Each week, check the calendar carefully for scheduling. Set aside time for chores around the house, being with people who are important to you and participating in an outside organization, such as a church or civic group. If you're striving for balance in your life, include time for exercise and recreation to keep your mind and body healthy, as well as to relieve stress.

Keep the household calendar where everyone can easily see what's scheduled for the day, week, month or even the year. As you add dates to the calendar, make certain these are things you really want to be involved in. It can be very easy to say "yes" to activities that aren't interesting or valuable to you. De-junk your life of activities by learning how to say "no."

A household calendar also makes it possible to check for proper balance in your life. You'll be able to see if you're spending too much time in one area and not enough in other important areas. For example, are you spending so much time exercising that you are helping others by being involved in a church or civic organization? Do you spend so much time with friends that you don't have enough time for your family? Evaluate your calendar at least once every six months to determine if you have balance in your life.

Do you keep a family calendar? If so, how do you use it? How could you use it better? Write your ideas here. If you don't keep one, make plans to start a family calendar as soon as possible.

Reflections

A house appointment

If you have a very active life, it's easy to forget about chores that need to be done around the house. That's why it's a good idea to make an appointment to do them. When tasks are scheduled for a specific day and time, they're more likely to get done. By de-junking your house first, chores will take less of your time and give you more time for things that are important to you.

Cleaning

In Chapter 3, I gave you some ideas for de-junking your personal space. When you're cleaning this saves time because you don't have so many things to wash, dust, vacuum or move. It'll also save time if you keep all of your cleaning supplies in a basket or other container so they're easy to move through the house. Choose one cleaning solution that will clean glass, counter tops, floors and other hard surfaces. This saves both time and money because you won't have to buy so many cleaning solutions.

In a two-story house, you'll save time if you keep cleaning supplies upstairs as well as downstairs. I even have two vacuums, one on each floor. That way, when I'm upstairs and have a few minutes, it's easy to grab the vacuum and make the most of that time. Another tip for a two-story house is to keep a basket on each floor. Anything that belongs on the other floor can be placed in the basket. At the end of the day take the basket to the right floor and put everything back where it belongs. This saves time and energy because you're not making lots of trips up and down the stairs just to put things away. If someone's missing an item, she can check the baskets before starting a full-scale search. This tip can save your family a lot frustration as well as time.

I've listed just some of the tasks that need to be done inside the house. Go outside and the list becomes even longer. Also consider the time it takes to care for your vehicles. Many families have two or more, which makes their maintenance even more time consuming.

The same organizational tips apply to the outside of your home. Keep tools in one general area of your garage or workshop. If you put tools back where they belong, you won't spend valuable time searching the next time you need them. Create a written or computerized schedule of when seasonal activities should be done — such as planting bulbs, fertilizing the grass, trimming the roses, washing windows or painting the house. When this schedule is posted where all family members can see it, everyone can plan more effectively. I can hear some of you saying, "Yeah, my kids would plan to be out of town that weekend." But at least you're teaching them to plan!

Go through your home and look at where you keep things. Ask yourself if this is the best place to keep an item based on its usage? Make a new list, rearranging things according to "usage determines storage."

Reflections

Lists for everything

Always make a list before going to the grocery store. This allows you to move quickly through the store since you know exactly what you need. You don't have to check every aisle for items you might need. With a list, several people can do the shopping together and get it done even faster.

Post the list where everyone in the house can see it and add items to it. The person who uses the last of something or notices when something is getting low should put it on the list. I keep my grocery list in a magnetic holder on the refrigerator. It includes cleaning supplies, light bulbs and other nonfood items as well as groceries. This way there's only one list to check when someone goes shopping. You could write your list on an envelope and then stick the coupons you'll use inside. This keeps everything together when you go shopping.

Another important list is a to-do list for your house. One family I know makes a list on the computer for the various household chores that need to be done each evening. This list's posted in the kitchen on Saturday morning and each person in the house signs his or her name next to particular tasks for that week. This adds variety to household chores and ensures that everyone knows what needs to be done. It also helps children develop a sense of responsibility and reminds them that living in a family means everyone contributes. In addition, it teaches them self-management skills as they learn to balance their activities with home responsibilities.

The two "Ps"

Conquering the two "Ps" is absolutely necessary if you're going to de-junk your time. The deadly Ps are very prominent in the lives of many people. Although some people suffer from only one of the Ps, it still junks up their lives. What are those two deadly Ps you ask? The two deadly Ps are procrastination and perfectionism. Let's look at procrastination first — otherwise we might put off dealing with perfectionism.

Dealing with procrastination

Since procrastination is a big time-waster, let me give you seven steps to overcome the habit.

1. Break large projects down into smaller projects. If you have several clearly defined pieces to an overwhelming project, this helps you conquer it. This also gives you confidence you can complete the project and that it's not going to take you the rest of your life.

2. Start with something you enjoy. This helps you get started because the first step is always the hardest. By breaking a large project into smaller ones, you can pick where to start. Some projects have to be completed in a certain order, but most of the time there are some small parts you can do right away in a short amount of time. This gets you moving on the project or activity.

3. Set a series of small, realistic deadlines instead of one final, large and looming deadline. This allows you to closely monitor your progress and stay on schedule.

4. Motivate yourself again and again by imagining the sense of accomplishment you'll feel when the project is finished. Set a goal of completing a specific part of the project before you take a break. Use small steps like this to keep you moving and motivated.

5. Make a conscious effort to remember your project won't be perfect. When you expect perfection, you set yourself up for failure. This is an unrealistic expectation and the leading cause of procrastination. When you give yourself permission to be less than perfect, it frees you to get the job done. (This is not an excuse to be sloppy but a reminder to be realistic.)

6. Get started now. Don't wait for a huge block of time because you may never find it. If you've broken the project into smaller projects, take advantage of your small blocks of time. If you spend

15 minutes today on the project, then you're 15 minutes closer to completing it.

7. Promise yourself a reward — and keep your promise. If you allow yourself small rewards along the way and a big reward when you finish, this gives you something to look forward to and a reason to feel good about yourself. You'll also be more eager to get on to the next section or part of the project.

These seven tips will help you get a grip on procrastination and begin to break the habit. They'll also help you get more done and get it done on time. Use these seven tips in both your personal and professional lives in order to be more effective.

What specific steps will you take to overcome procrastination on a specific project. Write them here.

The danger of perfectionism

As I mentioned earlier, perfectionism leads us to think that we can be perfect, and this is absolutely not true. We don't live in a perfect world. We aren't perfect, and we can't expect perfection of others or ourselves. It's an unrealistic expectation that junks up many people's lives. These people always strive to have the perfect home, the perfect outfit, the perfect family (whatever that might mean) or the perfect job. When they achieve less than perfection in any area, they become upset and discouraged. Striving for perfection can lead to constant complaining and even depression.

I've watched people set themselves up for failure because of their unrealistic expectations about the task they're attempting to complete and the amount of time they've set aside for it. They create stress for themselves and for the other people around them. Not only that, but they can't enjoy what they do or have because it's never perfect. In fact, their ideas may be so grandiose that the task will never be done on time or at all.

Learn to set realistic goals and be patient with yourself. Ask yourself the following questions:

1. Is there an easier way to do this project or activity?

2. Am I spending more time than this project deserves?

3. What are the consequences of using a simpler approach? (Consider both the positive and negative consequences.)

4. Am I missing out on something else equally important because I'm spending too much time on this project?

Realizing you're a perfectionist is the first step toward conquering it. Give yourself permission to make mistakes. If you set realistic time frames, you'll have time to correct mistakes. See each mistake as a learning experience. Remember that Thomas Edison tried over and over to invent the light bulb. However, each time he failed, he said he was one step closer to finding the right way to make a light bulb.

Also realize you can produce quality work without it being perfect. This is not an excuse to be careless. However, it's a caution to be realistic about the importance of the task and the time you spend on it.

The need to be perfect keeps many of you from trying to accomplish things you are more than capable of doing. If you suffer from perfectionism, select just one of your tasks and deliberately be good at it without trying to be perfect. You'll begin to experience a sense of freedom when you feel satisfied with who you are and what you're capable of doing. This doesn't mean you should never try to improve or grow. It does mean that not all tasks are worth the time, energy, effort and attention perfectionists give them. Carefully select where you spend your time and energy.

Do you suffer from perfectionism? If so, how does this affect your time and productivity? Refrain from creating a "tempest in a teapot" for nothing. Be willing to settle for less than perfect on your next project. How will you do that?

Reflections

Summary

To de-junk your time, always remember JAKE and use a family calendar and lists for shopping and jobs to be done. Don't let the two "Ps" of procrastination and perfectionism junk up your life either. Remind yourself that "Life is too short to be taken seriously." Enjoy the time you have by planning for the important things and saying no to things that aren't important. Here's JAKE Top Ten for conquering time at home.

JAKE's Top Ten

1. Have a family or household calendar where all major activities and dates are written down.

2. Keep the calendar in a central location where it's easy for everyone to see.

3. Make appointments to handle household chores — inside and outside.

4. Use lists — cleaning lists, grocery lists, project lists — to stay on track.

5. Keep supplies and tools together in moveable containers so they're easy to find and use.

6. Strive for balance in your life.

7. Start now to conquer procrastination by following the seven steps.

8. Realize everything isn't equally important. Leave the tyranny of perfectionism behind.

9. Schedule time to take care of yourself — spiritually, mentally, emotionally and physically.

10. Remember time is a precious gift — use it wisely by making choices instead of reacting to situations as they occur.

8 JAKE AND PRIORITIES — PROFESSIONAL AND PERSONAL

"Nothing is easier than being busy and nothing more difficult than being effective." Alec MacKenzie, a time-management author and consultant, is absolutely right. His words are a reminder that activity isn't the goal. It's easy to be busy and still not accomplish things that are most important in life. Everyone must set priorities because they're a reflection of how you'll spend your time. When you set priorities and follow through with goals and plans, you also de-junk your life. Setting priorities is the foundation of self-management in every area of your life. Self-management forces you to focus on your goals or what has to be accomplished.

When you know what's important to you and what your goals are, it's easy to say "no" to other activities that don't move you toward those goals. Setting priorities is a skill that anyone can master, but it takes desire and a willingness to invest time and energy. I'll deal with priorities in a general way because setting them works the same in both your professional and personal lives.

About 10 years ago, a friend of mine realized she didn't have any direction to her life. Cheryl was working six to seven days a week, without any goal other than survival. Her kids were out of control, and her husband had filed for divorce. She was challenged by some friends to begin taking control of her life — to decide what she wanted to accomplish. So she started making changes in her life. One of the first things she did was set some priorities. She decided where she wanted to be in five years and then created action plans to help her reach her goals.

As Cheryl got her life back on track she was able to concentrate on things that were really important to her. This paid off as she started spending more time with her children. As a result, they started doing better in school, and the relationship between Cheryl and her children improved. Six years later, she has a very successful business and is remarried. Her three children are well on their way to being successful adults. Cheryl was able to accomplish all this because she decided to take some specific steps to control her own life. She started by deciding where she wanted to go, then she set priorities and started moving toward them.

Going where?

To set priorities you must first know what you want to achieve. Take time right now to think about where you want to be in five years. Write down your answers to the following questions:

- What will you be doing?

- When will you be doing it?

- Where will you be doing it?

- Why will you be doing it?

- How will you be doing it?

- Whom will you be doing it with?

Answer these questions for both your professional life and your personal life. Use them to think about your vision for the future. Only when you have a picture of where you want to be in five years can you begin to create an action plan to take you there.

Don't be frustrated if you don't have a clear picture of where you want to be in five years. Begin to work on defining and refining your goals for life. Your goals will change over the years. However, if you don't start thinking about and setting your goals now, you'll end up somewhere, but it may not be where you wanted to be!

Once you've answered these questions, you can start creating action plans to accomplish your goals. Write your goals in pencil and don't be afraid to change them. Goals are guidelines for life. Circumstances change, lifestyles change, values change, interests change, and jobs change. Don't junk up your life by holding onto a goal that's not important to you anymore. Be willing to let go of that goal if it doesn't fit you now.

Setting goals and having a clear idea of where you want to go helps you make decisions that move you toward your goal. This makes it possible for you to manage yourself more effectively. Many people junk up their lives with worthwhile things that aren't part of the overall plan they have for their lives. My grandfather always used to say, "The good is the enemy of the best." You may need to eliminate some good things from your life because they keep you from concentrating on the best things for you.

Activity without goals junks up your professional life as well as your personal life. Professionally a person may not have a clear idea of where she wants to go in an organization or industry. Then she's surprised when someone else gets a promotion. She thinks, "That promotion should've been mine. I've been with the company longer than he has, and I can do the job." She probably can do the job. But since she didn't set professional goals for herself, she's just muddled along, hoping for the best. This type of person is constantly surprised when other people are "lucky." In most cases, this "luck" is the result of planning, preparing and working to achieve goals.

This is why I encourage people to think of themselves as self-employed. When you're self-employed, it's up to you to know where you're going and how you're going to get there. In today's world, even if you work for a large organization, you still need to take responsibility for where you're going professionally. People all over North America tell me they've been caught in downsized, right-sized or re-engineered organizations. They've been forced to deal with situations they never imagined or made plans to handle. So plan for your future — don't leave it to chance or the whim of someone else. It belongs to you, so set goals, establish priorities and take control of your life!

Some of you have clearly defined professional goals and then leave your personal life to chance. Without goals in your personal life, you can become involved in so many activities that you wear yourself out — you feel like your life is out of control. This leaves you frustrated and stressed. Having goals will help you keep your life in balance.

Stop and think about where you want to be in five years, three years and one year. What do you really want to achieve? Write some of your ideas down here.

Five years?

Three years?

One year?

Reflections

Setting goals for success

Setting goals is fun and exciting, however, it takes time and thought to come up with meaningful ones. Goals are a destination, something you should enjoy achieving. All your goals should be compatible so you have balance in your life. This helps de-junk your life of the activities that are no longer important to you. Once you accomplish one, set another and continue to move through life with purpose and direction. When you have goals, it's easy to be effective and not just busy.

You'll achieve balance in your life when you set goals in the following areas:

- Spiritual

- Family

- Friends

- Work

- Civic

- Financial

- Physical/recreational

- Mental growth

The order of their importance will vary for each person. When you have goals in each of these areas, it'll be easier for you to determine where to invest your time and energy. You'll have a clear picture of what's important to you and where you're going. By setting goals you're well on your way.

SMART goals

Goals should be written down. This gives them importance and makes them easy to refer to on a daily basis. So grab a piece of paper and start writing! If you're not familiar with setting goals, there are five components each goal should have. It's easy to remember these five by using the word SMART.

- S reminds us goals must be specific. The more specific the target, the more likely you are to hit it. Don't write "I'm going to get more done," because that isn't specific enough. Instead write "I'm going to accomplish these three projects this week," which is very specific.

- M is for measurable. You must know when you've accomplished the goal. If your goal is "to accomplish these three projects," then it's a measurable goal.

- A stands for action because a goal without an action plan is usually just a dream. How will you achieve this goal? What steps will you take to accomplish it? A possible action plan would be to work on this project on Monday, the second on Tuesday and the third on Wednesday.

- R means goals should be realistic. A goal should not be set so high that it discourages you. On the other hand, the goal should still be challenging and not easily achieved. A goal should offer a bit of a stretch for you so it provides you an opportunity to grow. For instance, you know it'll be tough to finish a project a day with your other responsibilities, but you're up for the challenge.

- T is a goal's time factor. What are your deadlines? What time factors have you assigned to this goal? Did you allow time for interruptions, gathering information, the possibility that people won't be available when they're needed and other circumstances that might come up? Did you allow for changes in your life situation?

Use SMART for both professional and personal goal-setting. This tool will help you de-junk your life of things that don't move you in the direction of your goals. It's much easier to say "no" when you keep focused on your goals and spend time only on the important things.

Think about each goal you set earlier. What steps do you have to take to arrive at its destination? Write your thoughts down here.

Reflections

Creating objectives

So you've written down some goals — now what? Just writing a goal down doesn't make it happen. You need a plan to achieve the goal. First determine what steps you'll need to take to accomplish your goal. These are objectives, which should always lead you toward your goal. An objective is a measure of accomplishment. It tells you where you are on your journey toward the goal. You'll achieve several objectives along the way to your goal, which is your final destination.

After you achieve this goal, set another and move on in life. Review your goals at least every six months to make sure they're still important to you. Don't set goals that are frustrating or totally unrealistic. Get rid of them, set new ones or revise the ones you have so they're still moving you in the right direction. This makes it easier to control priorities and gives you direction and balance in life.

Controlling priorities

Goal-setting helps you determine what's important and makes it possible for you to make informed decisions about your priorities. Priorities are a reflection of how you spend your time and manage yourself. Priorities help de-junk your life of unnecessary and unwanted commitments and activities.

Priorities can be divided into four categories:

- Urgent and important — the "fighting fires" category. If a payroll for 650 people is due in two hours and you haven't even started the process, this is both urgent and important.

- Not urgent and important — this must be done but not immediately. A presentation that must be made in two weeks is in this category.

- Urgent and not important — don't waste your energy on priorities like these that aren't important. A pre-approved credit-card application that must be returned in five days isn't important if you don't need a credit card. It doesn't matter how good the offer is, if you don't need it or it doesn't interest you.

- Not urgent and not important — because it's not important the urgency isn't a factor. For instance, you may not need a newspaper subscription because you don't have time to read a newspaper. If you do find the time someday, then you can always subscribe.

	Urgent	**Not Urgent**
Important	*Urgent & Important*	*Not Urgent & Important*
Not Important	*Urgent & Not Important*	*Not Urgent & Not Important*

Edwin Bliss, in his book *Getting Things Done*, classifies priorities using the ABC method. "Urgent and important" priorities are A priorities, which need your immediate attention. B priorities are "not urgent and important." They might be projects, objectives or long-range goals — anything you need to work on that doesn't have an immediate deadline. "Urgent and not important" and "not urgent and not important" shouldn't be bothered with since they have little or no value to you. These are C priorities.

- A priorities could be considered the "must do" items.

- B priorities are the "should do" items.

- C priorities are the "could do" items.

Spend most of your time on your A and B priorities. Look carefully at priorities considered urgent and important. Who considers this priority urgent and important? You? Your boss? A co-worker? Client or customer? Family member? Friend? Just because a priority is urgent and important to someone else doesn't mean it should be an A priority for you — unless of course that person is your boss, customer or an important person in your personal life. Concentrate on your A priorities and make time each day to work on some of your B priorities as well so you're moving steadily toward your goals.

Just as you set goals in each of the eight areas of life, you should set priorities in those same eight areas. This de-junks your life by helping you focus on the things that are most important to you. When you set goals, create objectives and prioritize in these eight areas, you'll find it easier to say no to things that aren't important to you anymore. You know where you're going and the steps you'll take to get there. You can be proactive rather than reactive because you also have an idea of the challenges facing you.

Focusing on priorities

Use the following questions to help you focus your energies on each of your priorities.

- What is my goal?

- What are my roles and responsibilities?

- What are my deadlines?

- How will I know that I've met my objectives?

- When I get what I want, what else in my life will improve?

- What might get worse?

- What resources do I have available to help me with this project?

- How can I best use these resources?

- What am I going to begin doing now to get what I want?

These questions make a great checklist to periodically monitor your progress toward the priorities you've set.

Create an action plan in the space below and then begin to work on it. Review your progress against your action plan every three to six months. On your calendar, make appointments to check on your progress.

Reflections

Clustering

If you're having a hard time setting your priorities use a technique called "clustering" or mind-mapping. With this technique don't be concerned about writing in complete sentences or trying to think of everything at once. There isn't a right or wrong way to cluster. It's just a technique to help you define your priorities, so grab a piece of paper and follow these steps:

1. Draw a picture, symbol and/or write a phrase in the center of the paper that represents you.

2. Write key words to define your priorities any place on the paper.

3. Take one main idea associated with a priority and branch out, drawing a picture or symbol or writing a key word or phrase.

4. Stop and think about that priority. Add new thoughts like branches on a tree.

5. Organize your thoughts by drawing lines and/or arrows to represent connections.

6. Use as much color and as many symbols and pictures as possible.

7. Use bold and capital letters; script writing is better than printing.

8. Don't crowd the page — leave space to add more ideas as they occur to you. Continue on another page if necessary.

In clustering use only key words. This isn't the time to write complete descriptions or sentences. When you see a key word, it'll remind you of the whole idea. Clustering allows you to see priorities in relationship to each other and gives you an opportunity to connect them. You also have the benefit of visualizing the priorities in your life, which can help you eliminate some of them. Take the time right now to do some clustering and be sure to include all eight areas of life:

- Spiritual

- Family

- Friends

- Work

- Civic

- Financial

- Physical/recreational

- Mental

Remember success isn't a matter of luck, but deciding what you want to do, planning how to succeed and then working through the challenges before you. What challenges do you have to deal with in order to reach one of your goals? Write down those challenges and include a plan to deal with each one of them.

Reflections
Reflections

The 80-20 Rule

JAKE de-junks priorities by concentrating on getting the most done in the least amount of time. He knows how important it is to be proactive. Proactive people are more productive with less effort and energy because they've learned to apply the 80-20 Rule. The 80-20 Rule (also called Pareto's Rule) states that 80 percent of our results come from 20 percent of our efforts.

Think about JAKE throughout your day. If you evaluate your time on a regular basis, you'll quickly see some activities give you only meager results even though you've expended a lot of effort. Eliminate those activities and concentrate on ones that pay off in a big way.

Often when you start a new project you'll see the 80-20 Rule in action. You experience a burst of energy and creativity that completes 80 percent of the project. Then you spend the rest of the time refining and perfecting it. Perfectionism violates the 80-20 Rule because you're constantly trying to improve the project. It may be more than adequate. You need to learn when to let go of a project and capture 80 percent of your results with 20 percent of your effort. If you do that consistently, you'll handle your priorities effectively and experience greater satisfaction. A side benefit will be the balance you have in your life because you're spending time on the important priorities, whether they're urgent or not. In other words, you're de-junking your priorities.

Just say "no"

There's an old Chinese proverb that sums it up pretty well. "Besides the noble art of getting things done, there is the noble art of leaving things undone. The wisdom of life lies in eliminating the nonessentials." Setting goals and establishing priorities guide you in what to leave undone and what to eliminate. You'll never be as effective as you could be if you don't learn to say "no" to the junk in your priorities and time. Remember JAKE — Junk Always Kills Effectiveness.

Not learning how to say "no" is something that defeats many of you. Your lives end up out of balance and out of control. There's not enough time to focus on your goals and priorities because you're letting someone else control you. It may be co-workers who like to chat on the job. It may be your children who constantly demand your attention at home. It may be over-commitments to a church or civic organization. It may be too many sports activities you're involved in. If that's the case, rely on JAKE who's always there to help you deal with the priorities in your life.

Summary

Once you decide where you want to be in five years, three years or even one year, you've taken a major step toward de-junking your life. At that point begin to set goals and create action plans based on your priorities. Using JAKE in your priorities gives you the ability to say "no" to anything that isn't essential to you and your life plan. This makes it easier to control your space, all of the information around you and your time because you have a clear view of where you're going. Here's JAKE's final Top Ten!

JAKE's Top Ten

1. Think of priorities as a reflection of how you spend your time, so knowing what's important to you is essential.

2. Develop and refine the skill of setting priorities.

3. Answer the "what, when, where, why, how and who" questions.

4. Use SMART goals to have bring balance to your life.

5. Set priorities and goals for the eight major areas of life.

6. Remember the four categories of priorities and concentrate on only the important ones.

7. Use clustering to regularly define and evaluate your goals and priorities.

8. Keep the 80-20 Rule in mind to help you achieve your goals.

9. Beware of the two Ps (procrastination and perfectionism). They're examples of junk that prevent you from achieving your priorities.

10. Follow the Chinese proverb: "Eliminate the nonessentials."

9 JAKE: JUNK ALWAYS KILLS EFFECTIVENESS

There are so many things you can do to de-junk your life. I hope this is the beginning of a great adventure for you and JAKE as you together declare war on junk and take control of your life. Use the information in this book — particularly JAKE's Top Ten lists at the end of each chapter — to begin de-junking. You'll have more balance and less stress in your life so you can spend time on the things you've decided are important.

JAKE leaves you with his master list of tips you can turn to at any time and use as a quick de-junking reference.

JAKE's Top Ten Plus Five

1. Use JAKE to take control of your life — it's all up to you! Realize this is a lifelong process.

2. Be yourself. Only use the de-junking and organizing tips that work best for you. Remember your left-brain/right-brain tendencies and take advantage of your strengths.

3. Answer the eight questions about evaluating your workspace at least once a year.

4. If you don't use it, dump it!

5. Remember usage determines storage. Always think about how you'll use something before you think about where to store it.

6. Use directories, subdirectories and simple file names to keep your computer files under control.

7. Use the Internet as a source for current, up-to-date information.

8. Have a plan to keep your personal business papers and related information easy to use, accessible and under control.

9. Use only one calendar to keep track of both your professional and personal information and activities.

10. Make your most important appointment of the day your 10-to-15 minute planning appointment. This helps you get the best results from your day.

11. Use a master list, to-do list and checklists to stay on target with your time.

12. Set up a tickler file to keep all upcoming information in one location. This can be effective for both your professional and personal lives.

13. Keep the two "Ps" (procrastination and perfectionism) under control or they can destroy your effectiveness.

14. Establish your vision for five years, three years and one year. Then use goals, action plans and priorities to move toward them.

15. Rely on JAKE, the happy warrior, who's your greatest ally in the war on junk.

By following these 15 tips you'll bring balance to your life, reduce stress, become more productive and gain a sense of control over your time. As JAKE would say, "Happy de-junking!"

I INDEX

Notes

Notes

Notes

Notes

Notes

Notes

Buy any 3, get 1 FREE!

Get a 60-Minute Training Series™ Handbook FREE ($14.95 value)* when you buy any three. See back of order form for full selection of titles.

These are helpful how-to books for you, your employees and co-workers. Add to your library. Use for new-employee training, brown-bag seminars, promotion gifts and more. Choose from many popular titles on a variety of lifestyle, communication, productivity and leadership topics. Exclusively from National Press Publications.

BUY 3 GET 1 FREE! Buy more, save more!

DESKTOP HANDBOOK ORDER FORM

Ordering is easy:

1. Complete both sides of this Order Form, detach, and mail, fax or phone your order to:

    Mail: National Press Publications
    P.O. Box 419107
    Kansas City, MO 64141-6107

    Fax: 1-913-432-0824
    Phone: 1-800-258-7248
    Internet: www.natsem.com

2. Please print:

    Name_____ Position/Title _____

    Company/Organization_____

    Address_____City _____

    State/Province_____ZIP/Postal Code _____

    Telephone (____)_____ Fax (____) _____

    Your e-mail: _____

3. Easy payment:

    ❏ Enclosed is my check or money order for $_____ (total from back).
    Please make payable to National Press Publications.

    Please charge to:
    ❏ MasterCard   ❏ VISA   ❏ American Express

    Credit Card No. _____ Exp. Date_____

    Signature_____

• •

MORE WAYS TO SAVE:

SAVE 33%!!! BUY 20-50 COPIES of any title ... pay just $9.95 each ($11.25 Canadian).

SAVE 40%!!! BUY 51 COPIES OR MORE of any title ... pay just $8.95 each ($10.25 Canadian).

* $20.00 in Canada

Buy 3, get 1 FREE!
60-MINUTE TRAINING SERIES™ HANDBOOKS

TITLE	RETAIL PRICE	QTY	TOTAL
8 Steps for Highly Effective Negotiations #424	$14.95		
Assertiveness #4422	$14.95		
Balancing Career and Family #4152	$14.95		
Common Ground #4122	$14.95		
Delegate for Results #4592	$14.95		
The Essentials of Business Writing #4310	$14.95		
Everyday Parenting Solutions #4862	$14.95		
Exceptional Customer Service #4882	$14.95		
Fear & Anger: Slay the Dragons … #4302	$14.95		
Fundamentals of Planning #4301	$14.95		
Getting Things Donc #4112	$14.95		
How to Coach an Effective Team #4308	$14.95		
How to De-Junk Your Life #4306	$14.95		
How to Handle Conflict and Confrontation #4952	$14.95		
How to Manage Your Boss #493	$14.95		
How to Supervise People #4102	$14.95		
How to Work With People #4032	$14.95		
Inspire & Motivate: Performance Reviews #4232	$14.95		
Listen Up: Hear What's Really Being Said #4172	$14.95		
Motivation and Goal-Setting #4962	$14.95		
A New Attitude #4432	$14.95		
The New Dynamic Comm. Skills for Women #4309	$14.95		
The Polished Professional #4262	$14.95		
The Power of Innovative Thinking #428	$14.95		
The Power of Self-Managed Teams #4222	$14.95		
Powerful Communication Skills #4132	$14.95		
Present With Confidence #4612	$14.95		
The Secret to Developing Peak Performers #4692	$14.95		
Self-Esteem: The Power to Be Your Best #4642	$14.95		
Shortcuts to Organized Files & Records #4307	$14.95		
The Stress Management Handbook #4842	$14.95		
Supreme Teams: How to Make Teams Work #4303	$14.95		
Thriving on Change #4212	$14.95		
Women and Leadership #4632	$14.95		

Sales Tax

All purchases subject to state and local sales tax.
Questions?
Call
1-800-258-7248

Subtotal	$	
Add 7% Sales Tax (*Or add appropriate state and local tax*)	$	
Shipping and Handling (*$3 one item; 50¢ each additional item*)	$	
TOTAL	$	

08/01